Readings in Literary Criticism 15
CRITICS ON DRYDEN

Readings in Literary Criticism

1. CRITICS ON KEATS
2. CRITICS ON CHARLOTTE AND EMILY BRONTE
3. CRITICS ON POPE
4. CRITICS ON MARLOWE
5. CRITICS ON JANE AUSTEN   Edited by Judith O'Neill
6. CRITICS ON CHAUCER   Edited by Sheila Sullivan
7. CRITICS ON BLAKE   Edited by Judith O'Neill
8. CRITICS ON VIRGINIA WOOLF   Edited by Jacqueline Latham
9. CRITICS ON D. H. LAWRENCE   Edited by W. T. Andrews
10. CRITICS ON YEATS   Edited by Raymond Cowell
11. CRITICS ON MATTHEW ARNOLD   Edited by Jacqueline Latham
12. CRITICS ON WORDSWORTH   Edited by Raymond Cowell
13. CRITICS ON GEORGE ELIOT   Edited by William Baker
14. CRITICS ON T. S. ELIOT   Edited by Sheila Sullivan
15. CRITICS ON DRYDEN   Edited by Robert McHenry and David G. Lougee

CRITICS ON DRYDEN

Readings in Literary Criticism

Edited by Robert McHenry and
David G. Lougee

London · George Allen and Unwin Ltd

ISBN 0 04 821031 5

PRINTED IN GREAT BRITAIN
in 10 point Plantin type
BY CLARKE, DOBLE & BRENDON LTD
PLYMOUTH

CONTENTS

INTRODUCTION   *page*   vi

ACKNOWLEDGEMENTS   viii

CRITICS ON DRYDEN 1717–1920

JOHN DENNIS	John Dryden	I
WILLIAM CONGREVE	On Dryden's Character and Writings	I
SAMUEL JOHNSON	Life of Dryden	3
WILLIAM WORDSWORTH	Letter to Walter Scott	7
HENRY HALLAM	John Dryden	8
WILLIAM HAZLITT	On Dryden and Pope	8
THOMAS BABINGTON MACAULAY	John Dryden	10
HIPPOLYTE TAINE	The Classic Age: Dryden	11
MATTHEW ARNOLD	The Study of Poetry: Dryden and Pope	13
JAMES RUSSELL LOWELL	Dryden	14
MARK VAN DOREN	The Poetry of John Dryden	16

MODERN CRITICS ON DRYDEN

EARL MINER	Dryden and the Issue of Human Progress	19
ARTHUR W. HOFFMAN	*Absalom and Achitophel*	28
ALAN ROPER	Analogies for Poetry	45
BRUCE KING	*All for Love*	57
PHILLIP HARTH	The Sceptical Critic	63
JOEL BLAIR	Dryden's Ceremonial Hero	76
ROBERT D. HUME	The Essay *Of Dramatic Poesy*	89
THOMAS H. FUJIMURA	The Personal Drama of Dryden's *The Hind and the Panther*	95

SELECT BIBLIOGRAPHY   III

INTRODUCTION

Dryden's reputation has been far from stable in the three centuries since he wrote. Indeed, even those critics who have praised his literary achievements have often done so with heavy qualifications. Many who have praised his style have attacked his character and principles and the 'immorality' of much of his writing. Most seem to have agreed that Dryden brought about a revolution in poetic practice, but at the same time they have considered him only one of the better second-rate poets. Most have found him the pre-eminent poet of the intellect, but they have asserted that his 'poetry of statement' does not express passion. Some have even asserted that his poetry is not poetry at all, but prose. Only relatively recently have critics, by applying new critical approaches to Dryden's work, effected an expanded and favourable re-evaluation of his achievements.

This collection of critical essays on Dryden's writings, especially his poetry, tries to give some sense of the vicissitudes of Dryden's reputation by offering a brief sample of influential and original older criticism. It also seeks to provide a collection of recent essays that demonstrate fruitful approaches to some of Dryden's major works and to a variety of issues raised by his poetry, drama and criticism.

The first section of the book contains short but representative selections from critics writing between 1717 and 1920. Both William Congreve and John Dennis knew Dryden personally, and while they did not offer praise lightly, they wrote highly complimentary accounts of Dryden's character and talents. Samuel Johnson's brilliant discussions have been the most influential writings on Dryden of all time and indeed became in the nineteenth century the starting point for most evaluations of Dryden's work. Henry Hallam, Thomas Babington Macaulay, and Hippolyte Taine represent the curious duality of many nineteenth-century views of Dryden: they often condemn vigorously his ideas and person while they praise his literary importance and certain aspects of his style. William Wordsworth and, especially, Matthew Arnold judge Dryden severely, finding him no poet at all but a 'classic of our prose'. The pieces from James Russell Lowell and Mark Van Doren reflect the tendency to praise Dryden but to relegate him nonetheless to a secondary importance in literary history: he was a 'genius', as T. S. Eliot wrote, but he had a 'commonplace mind'.

The modern critical essays in the second section exemplify the most influential recent criticism not found in other critical anthologies on Dryden's work. They suggest the variety of rewarding approaches to Dryden's literary and critical art. Our understanding and appreciation, for instance, of the relationship between Dryden's poetry and the intellectual climate which nourished it have been increased by the history-of-ideas approach of both Phillip Harth, who has established Dryden's connection with the central rationalism of the Anglican

Church and with the 'scepticism' of the Royal Society, and Earl Miner, who has placed Dryden in the context of the seventeenth-century debate about human progress. Other critics have examined Dryden's use of certain neoclassical poetic techniques with a New-Critical closeness: Arthur Hoffman's essay demonstrates the controlled richness of Dryden's imagery in 'Absalom and Achitophel', and Alan Roper's explanation of the term 'analogy' helps to distinguish Dryden's characteristic use of metaphors from that of other poets. Joel Blair's essay combines a close reading of several of Dryden's poems with an attempt to show how Dryden's concept of the hero reflects his social and political ideas. And lastly, Thomas Fujimura's article establishes a new approach to what has been regarded as a poem of 'ratiocination' by clarifying Dryden's personal involvement in the debate between the Hind and the Panther.

Just as some recent critics have rediscovered Dryden's poetry, others have brought new analysis and evaluation to Dryden's plays and his literary criticism. Bruce King's study of *All for Love* shows Dryden's concern for the passions in his serious drama, and Robert D. Hume discusses 'Of Dramatic Poesy' as part of a complex evolution of Dryden's critical values away from contemporary demands for literal imitation in drama.

The modern criticism from which these essays have been selected is significant because new critical approaches have proved the necessary prelude to the modern upward re-evaluation of Dryden's achievement. Nineteenth-century critics grew increasingly hostile to Dryden because they seemed locked into the approaches to his poetry established by Samuel Johnson in the eighteenth century, even though they dissented from Johnson's literary and social values. As a result they saw only what Johnson saw, but what he admired, they hated. Thus recent criticism has allowed students to see—and admire—more of Dryden's art.

Because the essays here are complete or substantially complete, including their methods and evidence as well as their conclusions, and because of limitations of space, many excellent articles have been of necessity excluded. The bibliography at the end of the book indicates some of the other fine articles and books on Dryden's work. We hope that this collection will stimulate students to explore further the riches of Dryden.

ROBERT MCHENRY
University of Hawaii

DAVID G. LOUGEE
Florida State University

ACKNOWLEDGEMENTS

We wish to thank the following for permission to reprint copyright material from the works listed below.

Johns Hopkins Press ('Remarks upon Mr Pope's Translation of Homer' from *Critical Works of John Dennis*, edited by E. N. Hooker); Macmillan Co. (*William Congreve: Letters and Documents*, edited by John C. Hodges); The Clarendon Press (Samuel Johnson, *Lives of the English Poets*, edited by George Birbeck Hill, 1905, Vols 1 and 3; One letter from *The Letters of William and Dorothy Wordsworth*, edited by Ernest de Selincourt, revised by Chester L. Shaver, 2nd edition, 1967, Vol. 1); Constable and Co. (Henry Hallam's 'A Review of Scott's edition of Dryden's *Works*' from *Edinburgh Review*, Vol. 13, 1809); Houghton Mifflin Company (James Russell Lowell's 'Dryden' from *Among My Books*); Oxford University Press (William Hazlitt's 'Lecture IV: on Dryden and Pope' from *Lectures on English Poets*); A. M. Heath and Company Ltd (Mark Van Doren's *John Dryden: A Study of His Poetry*); University of Iowa Press (Earl Miner's 'Dryden and the Issue of Human Progress' from *Philological Quarterly*, Vol. 40, No. 1, 1961); University of Florida Press (Arthur W. Hoffman's *John Dryden's Imagery*); Routledge and Kegan Paul Ltd (Alan Roper's *Dryden's Poetic Kingdoms*); Oliver and Boyd (Bruce King's *Dryden's Major Plays*); University of Chicago Press (Phillip Harth's *Contexts of Dryden's Thought*); Studies in English Literature (Joel Blair's 'Dryden's Ceremonial Hero' from *Studies in English Literature*, Vol. 9, No. 3, 1969); Cornell University Press (Robert D. Hume's *Dryden's Criticism*, © 1970 by Cornell University); Modern Language Association of America (Thomas H. Fujimura's 'The Personal Drama of Dryden's "The Hind and the Panther"' from *PMLA*, May 1972).

Critics on Dryden
1717-1920

JOHN DENNIS: 1717

John Dryden

Mr Dryden, who had so many great Qualities, who refin'd the Language of our Rhyming Poetry, and improv'd its Harmony, who thought often, so finely, so justly, so greatly, so nobly, who had the Art of Reasoning very strongly in very elegant Verse; and who of all our Rhyming Poets wrote beyond comparison with most Force, and with most Elevation; was often sacrific'd to his worthless Contemporaries; could never receive Encouragement enough to set him entirely at Ease, died without leaving behind him enough to inter him, and left behind him a destitute and deplorable Family.

> From 'Remarks upon Mr Pope's Translation of Homer', in *Critical Works of John Dennis*, ed. E. N. Hooker, 2 vols, Baltimore, 1939–43, Vol. 2, pp. 115–58 (121).
> [In these footnotes of sources, the first page numbers represent the entire article or section; the numbers in parentheses are of the pages chosen in our selection.]

WILLIAM CONGREVE: 1717

On Dryden's Character and Writings

He was of a Nature exceedingly Humane and Compassionate; easily forgiving Injuries, and capable of a prompt and sincere Reconciliation with them who had offended him.

Such a Temperament is the only solid Foundation of all moral Virtues, and sociable Endowments. His Friendship, where he profess'd it, went much beyond his Professions; and I have been told of strong and generous Instances of it, by the Persons themselves who received them: Tho' his Hereditary Income was little more than a bare Competency.

As his Reading had been very extensive, so was he very happy in a Memory tenacious of every thing that he had read. He was not more possess'd of Knowledge than he was Communicative of it. But then his Communication of it was by no means pedantick, or impos'd upon the Conversation; but just such, and went so far as by the natural Turns of the Discourse in which he was engag'd it was necessarily promoted or required. He was extream ready and gentle in his Correction of the Errors of any Writer, who thought fit to consult him; and full as ready and patient to admit of the Reprehension of others in respect of his own Oversight or Mistakes. He was of very easy, I may say of very pleasing Access: But something slow, and as it were diffident in his Advances to others. He had something in his Nature that abhorr'd Intrusion into any Society whatsoever. Indeed it is to be regretted, that he was rather blameable in the other Extream: For by that means, he was Personally less known, and consequently his Character might become liable both to Misapprehensions and Misrepresentations.

To the best of my Knowledge and Observation, he was, of all the Men that ever I knew, one of the most Modest, and the most Easily to be discountenanced, in his Approaches, either to his Superiors, or his Equals.

I have given Your Grace this slight Sketch of his personal Character, as well to vindicate his Memory, as to justify my self for the Love which I bore to his Person; and I have the rather done it, because I hope it may be acceptable to You to know that he was worthy of the Distinction You have shewn him, as a Man, as well as an Author.

As to his Writings, I shall not take upon me to speak of them; for, to say little of them, would not be to do them right: And to say all that I ought to say, would be, to be very Voluminous. But, I may venture to say in general Terms, that no Man hath written in our Language so much, and so various Matter, and in so various Manners, so well. Another thing I may say very peculiar to him; which is, that his Parts did not decline with his Years: But that he was an improving Writer to his last, even to near seventy Years of Age; improving even in Fire and Imagination, as well as in Judgement: Witness his Ode on St *Cecelia*'s Day, and his Fables, his latest Performances.

He was equally excellent in Verse, and in Prose. His Prose had all the Clearness imaginable, together with all the Nobleness of Expression; all the Graces and Ornaments proper and peculiar to it, without deviating into the Language or Diction of Poetry. I make this Observation, only to distinguish his Stile from that of many Poetical Writers, who meaning to write harmoniously in Prose, do in truth often write meer Blank Verse.

I have heard him frequently own with Pleasure, that if he had any Talent for *English* Prose, it was owing to his having often read the Writings of the great Archbishop *Tillotson*.

His Versification and his Numbers he could learn of no Body: For he first possess'd those Talents in Perfection in our Tongue. And they who have best succeeded in them since his Time, have been indebted to his Example; and the more they have been able to imitate him, the better they have succeeded.

As his Stile in Prose is always specifically different from his Stile in Poetry; so, on the other hand, in his Poems, his Diction is, wherever his Subject requires it, so Sublimely, and so truly Poetical that its Essence, like that of pure Gold, cannot be destroy'd. Take his Verses, and divest them of their Rhimes, disjoint them in their Numbers, transpose their Expressions, make what Arrangement and Disposition you please of his Words, yet shall there Eternally be Poetry, and something which will be found incapable of being resolv'd into absolute Prose: An incontestable Characteristick of a truly poetical Genius.

I will say but one Word more in general of his Writings, which is, that what he has done in any one Species, or distinct Kind, would have been sufficient to have acquir'd him a great Name. If he had written nothing but his Prefaces, or nothing but his Songs, or his Prologues, each of them would have intituled him to the Preference and Distinction of excelling in his Kind.

From 'Epistle Dedicatory to Thomas Pelham-Holles, Duke of Newcastle', in *William Congreve: Letters and Documents*, ed. John C. Hodges, New York, 1964, pp. 124–9 (127–9).

SAMUEL JOHNSON: 1779–1781

Life of Dryden

His literature, though not always free from ostentation, will be commonly found either obvious, and made his own by the art of dressing it; or superficial, which by what he gives shews what he wanted; or erroneous, hastily collected, and negligently scattered.

Yet it cannot be said that his genius is ever unprovided of matter, or that his fancy languishes in penury of ideas. His works abound with knowledge, and sparkle with illustrations. There is scarcely any science or faculty that does not supply him with occasional images and lucky similitudes; every page discovers a mind very widely acquainted both with art and nature, and in full possession of great stores of intellectual wealth. Of him that knows much it is natural to suppose that he has read with diligence; yet I rather believe that the knowledge of Dryden was gleaned from accidental intelligence and various conversation; by a quick apprehension, a judicious selection, and a happy memory, a keen appetite of knowledge, and a powerful digestion; by vigilance that permitted nothing to pass without notice, and a habit of reflection that suffered nothing useful to be lost. A mind like Dryden's, always curious, always active, to which every understanding was proud to be associated, and of which every one solicited the regard by an ambitious display of himself, had a more pleasant, perhaps a nearer, way to knowledge than by the silent progress of solitary reading. I do not suppose that he despised books or intentionally neglected them; but that he was carried out by the impetuosity of his genius to more vivid and speedy instructors, and that his studies were rather desultory and fortuitous than constant and systematical. . . .

In a general survey of Dryden's labours he appears to have had a mind very comprehensive by nature, and much enriched with acquired knowledge. His compositions are the effects of a vigorous genius operating upon large materials.

The power that predominated in his intellectual operations was rather strong reason than quick sensibility. Upon all occasions that were presented he studied rather than felt, and produced sentiments not such as Nature enforces, but meditation supplies. With the simple and elemental passions, as they spring separate in the mind, he seems not much acquainted, and seldom describes them but as they are complicated by the various relations of society and confused in the tumults and agitations of life.

What he says of love may contribute to the explanation of his character:

Love various minds does variously inspire;
It stirs in gentle bosoms [natures] gentle fire,
Like that of incense on the altar [altars] laid;
But raging flames tempestuous souls invade,
A fire which every windy passion blows;
With pride it mounts, or [and] with revenge it glows.

Dryden's was not one of the 'gentle bosoms': Love, as it subsists in itself, with no tendency but to the person loved and wishing only for correspondent kindness, such love as shuts out all other interest, the Love of the Golden Age, was too soft and subtle to put his faculties in motion. He hardly conceived it but in its turbulent effervescence with some other desires: when it was inflamed by rivalry or obstructed by difficulties; when it invigorated ambition or exasperated revenge.

He is therefore, with all his variety of excellence, not often pathetick; and had so little sensibility of the power of effusions purely natural that he did not esteem them in others. Simplicity gave him no pleasure; and for the first part of his life he looked on Otway with contempt, though at last, indeed very late, he confessed that in his play 'there was Nature, which is the chief beauty'.

We do not always know our own motives. I am not certain whether it was not rather the difficulty which he found in exhibiting the genuine operations of the heart than a servile submission to an injudicious audience that filled his plays with false magnificence. It was necessary to fix attention; and the mind can be captivated only by recollection or by curiosity; by reviving natural sentiments or impressing new appearances of things: sentences were readier at his call than images; he could more easily fill the ear with some splendid novelty than awaken those ideas that slumber in the heart.

The favourite exercise of his mind was ratiocination; and, that argument might not be too soon at an end, he delighted to talk of liberty and necessity, destiny and contingence; these he discusses in the language of the school with so much profundity that the terms which he uses are not always understood. It is indeed learning, but learning out of place.

When once he had engaged himself in disputation, thoughts flowed in on either side: he was now no longer at a loss; he had always objections and solutions at command: *'verbaque provisam rem'*—give him matter for his verse, and he finds without difficulty verse for his matter.

In comedy, for which he professes himself not naturally qualified, the mirth which he excites will perhaps not be found so much to arise from any original humour or peculiarity of character nicely distinguished and diligently pursued, as from incidents and circumstances, artifices and surprises; from jests of action rather than of sentiment. What he had of humorous or passionate, he seems to have had not from nature, but from other poets; if not always as a plagiary, at least as an imitator.

Next to argument, his delight was in wild and daring sallies of sentiment, in the irregular and excentrick violence of wit. He delighted to tread upon the brink of meaning, where light and darkness begin to mingle; to approach the precipice of absurdity, and hover over the abyss of unideal vacancy. This inclination sometimes produced nonsense, which he knew, as

Move swiftly, sun, and fly a lover's pace,
Leave weeks and months behind thee in thy race.
            Amariel flies . . .
To guard thee from the demons of the air;
My flaming sword above them to display,
All keen, and ground upon the edge of day.

And sometimes it issued in absurdities, of which perhaps he was not conscious:

Then we upon our orb's last verge shall go,
    And see the ocean leaning on the sky;
From thence our rolling neighbours we shall know,
    And on the lunar world securely pry.

These lines have no meaning; but may we not say, in imitation of Cowley on another book,

'Tis so like *sense* 'twill serve the turn as well? . . .

. . . His faults of negligence are beyond recital. Such is the unevenness of his compositions that ten lines are seldom found together without something of which the reader is ashamed. Dryden was no rigid judge of his own pages; he seldom struggled after supreme excellence, but snatched in haste what was within his reach; and when he could content others, was himself contented. He did not keep present to his mind an idea of pure perfection; nor compare his works, such as they were, with what they might be made. He knew to whom he should be opposed. He had more musick than Waller, more vigour than Denham, and more nature than Cowley; and from his contemporaries he was in no danger.

Standing therefore in the highest place he had no care to rise by contending with himself; but while there was no name above his own was willing to enjoy fame on the easiest terms.

He was no lover of labour. What he thought sufficient he did not stop to make better, and allowed himself to leave many parts unfinished, in confidence that the good lines would overbalance the bad. What he had once written he dismissed from his thoughts; and, I believe, there is no example to be found of any correction or improvement made by him after publication. The hastiness of his productions might be the effect of necessity; but his subsequent neglect could hardly have any other cause than impatience of study.

What can be said of his versification will be little more than a dilatation of the praise given it by Pope:

> Waller was smooth; but Dryden taught to join
> The varying verse, the full-resounding line,
> The long majestick march, and energy divine.

Some improvements had been already made in English numbers, but the full force of our language was not yet felt: the verse that was smooth was commonly feeble. If Cowley had sometimes a finished line he had it by chance. Dryden knew how to chuse the flowing and the sonorous words; to vary the pauses and adjust the accents; to diversify the cadence, and yet preserve the smoothness of his metre. . . .

Of Dryden's works it was said by Pope that 'he could select from them better specimens of every mode of poetry than any other English writer could supply'. Perhaps no nation ever produced a writer that enriched his language with such variety of models. To him we owe the improvement, perhaps the completion of our metre, the refinement of our language, and much of the correctness of our sentiments. By him we were taught *'sapere et fari'*, to think naturally and express forcibly. Though Davies has reasoned in rhyme before him, it may be perhaps maintained that he was the first who joined argument with poetry. He shewed us the true bounds of a translator's liberty. What was said of Rome, adorned by Augustus, may be applied by an easy metaphor to English poetry embellished by Dryden, *'lateritiam invenit, marmoream reliquit'*, he found it brick, and he left it marble.

From 'Life of Pope'

Of genius, that power which constitutes a poet; that quality without which judgement is cold and knowledge is inert; that energy which collects, combines, amplifies, and animates—the superiority must, with some hesitation, be allowed to Dryden [over Pope]. It is not to be inferred that of this poetical vigour Pope had only a little, because Dryden had more, for every other writer since Milton must give place to Pope; and even of Dryden it must be said that if he has brighter paragraphs, he has not better poems. Dryden's performances were always hasty, either excited by some external occasion, or extorted by domestick necessity; he composed without consideration, and published without correction. What his mind could supply at call, or gather in one excursion, was all that he sought, and all that he gave. The dilatory caution of Pope enabled him to condense his sentiments, to multiply his images, and to accumulate all that study might produce, or chance might supply. If the flights of Dryden therefore are higher, Pope continues longer on the wing. If of Dryden's fire the blaze is brighter, of Pope's the heat is more regular and constant. Dryden often surpasses expectation, and Pope never falls below it. Dryden is read with frequent astonishment, and Pope with perpetual delight.

From *Lives of the English Poets*, ed. George Birkbeck Hill, 3 Vols, Oxford, 1905, Vol. 1, pp. 417–69 (417, 457–61, 464–6, 469) and Vol. 3, pp. 82–276 (222–3).

WILLIAM WORDSWORTH: 1805

Letter to Walter Scott

I was much pleased to hear of your engagement with Dryden:[1] not that he is, as a *Poet*, any great favourite of mine: I admire his talents and Genius greatly, but his is not a poetical Genius: the only qualities I can find in Dryden that are *essentially* poetical are a certain ardour and impetuosity of mind with an excellent ear: it may seem strange that I do not add to this, great command of language: *that* he certainly has and of such language also as it is most desirable that a Poet should possess, or rather should not be without; but it is not language that is in the high sense of the word poetical, being neither of the imagination or the passions; I mean of the amiable the ennobling or intense passions; I do not mean to say that there is nothing of this in Dryden, but as little, I think, as is possible, considering how much he has written. You will easily understand my meaning when I refer to his versification of Palamon and Arcite as contrasted with the language of Chaucer.[2] Dryden had neither a tender heart nor a lofty sense of moral dignity: where his language is poetically impassioned it is mostly upon unpleasing subjects; such as the follies, vice, and crimes of classes of men or of individuals. That his cannot be the language of the imagination must have necessarily followed from this, that there is not a single image from Nature in the whole body of his works; and in his translation from Vergil whenever Vergil can be fairly said to have had his *eye* upon his object, Dryden always spoils the passage.

From *The Letters of William and Dorothy Wordsworth*, ed. Ernest De Selincourt, 2nd ed., Oxford, 1967, Vol. 1, pp. 640–1 (641).

---

[1] Scott's *The Works of John Dryden Now First Collected* was published in 1808 in eighteen volumes.
[2] The first item in his *Fables* (1700).

B

HENRY HALLAM: 1809

John Dryden

The leading feature of this great poet's mind was its rapidity of concep-
tion, combined with that, which is the excellence of some great painters,
—a readiness of expressing every idea, without losing anything by the
way. Whatever he does, whether he reasons, relates, or describes, he is
never, to use his own phrase, *cursedly confined*; never loiters about a
single thought or image, or seems to labour about the turn of a phrase.
Though he has many slovenly and feeble lines, perhaps scarce any
poet has so few which have failed for want of power to make them better.
He never, like Pope, forces an awkward rhyme, or spins out a couplet
for the sake of the pointed conclusion. His thoughts, his language, his
versification, have all a certain animation and elasticity, which no one
else has ever equally possessed. . . .

The pleasure which we receive from Dryden's poetry is more
exclusively due to him, because he was seldom much assisted by his
subject. In varied and interesting narratives, in tragedies which excite
emotion by their incidents, it is a matter of curious and difficult analysis,
to separate the merit of the artist from the richness of the materials. But
Dryden wrought commonly without much selection, and felt a confi-
dence that any subject would become poetical under his hand. He had,
indeed, no choice in his satires; yet there is surely nothing well conceived
or well conducted in the allegory of Absalom and Achitophel. . . . But
nothing can be more preposterous than the allegory of the Hind and
Panther; nor are the fancies of a dream more confused, than the con-
tinual changes to and fro between the language of wild beasts and of
churchmen.

From a review of Scott's edition of the *Works* of Dryden, *Edinburgh
Review*, Vol. 13, 1809, pp. 116–35 (132–3).

WILLIAM HAZLITT: 1818

On Dryden and Pope

Dryden and Pope are the great masters of the artificial style of poetry in
our language, as the poets of whom I have already treated, Chaucer,
Spenser, Shakespeare, and Milton, were of the natural; and though
this artificial style is generally and very justly acknowledged to be
inferior to the other, yet those who stand at the head of that class,
ought, perhaps to rank higher than those who occupy an inferior place
in a superior class. They have a clear and independent claim upon our
gratitude, as having produced a kind and degree of excellence which
existed equally nowhere else. What has been done well by some later
writers of the highest style of poetry, is included in, and obscured by a

greater degree of power and genius in those before them: what has been done best by poets of an entirely distinct turn of mind, stands by itself, and tells for its whole amount. Young, for instance, Gray, or Akenside, only follow in the train of Milton and Shakespeare: Pope and Dryden walk by their side, though of an unequal stature, and are entitled to a first place in the lists of fame. This seems to be not only the reason of the thing, but the common sense of mankind, who, without any regular process of reflection, judge of the merit of a work, not more by its inherent and absolute worth, than by its originality and capacity of gratifying a different faculty of the mind, or a different class of readers; for it should be recollected, that there may be readers (as well as poets) not of the highest class, though very good sort of people, and not altogether to be despised. . . .

Dryden was a better prose writer, and a bolder and more varied versifier than Pope. He was a more vigorous thinker, a more correct and logical declaimer, and had more of what may be called strength of mind than Pope; but he had not the same refinement and delicacy of feeling. Dryden's eloquence and spirit were possessed in a higher degree by others, and in nearly the same degree by Pope himself; but that by which Pope was distinguished, was an essence which he alone possessed, and of incomparable value on that sole account. Dryden's *Epistles* are excellent, but inferior to Pope's though they appear (particularly the admirable one to Congreve) to have been the model on which the latter formed his. His *Satires* are better than Pope's. His *Absalom and Achitophel* is superior, both in force of invective and discrimination of character, to anything of Pope's in the same way. The character of Achitophel is very fine; and breathes, if not a sincere love for virtue, a strong spirit of indignation against vice.

Mac Flecknoe is the origin of the idea of the *Dunciad*; but it is less elaborately constructed, less feeble, and less heavy. The difference between Pope's satirical portraits and Dryden's, appears to be this in a good measure, that Dryden seems to grapple with his antagonists, and to describe real persons; Pope seems to refine upon them in his own mind, and to make them out just what he pleases, till they are not real characters, but the mere drivelling effusions of his spleen and malice. Pope describes the thing, and then goes on describing his own description till he loses himself in verbal repetitions. Dryden recurs to the object often, takes fresh sittings of nature, and gives us new strokes of character as well as of his pencil. The *Hind and Panther* is an allegory as well as a satire; and so far it tells less home; the battery is not so point-blank. But otherwise it has more genius, vehemence, and strength of description than any other of Dryden's works, not excepting the *Absalom and Achitophel*. It also contains the finest examples of varied and sounding versification.

From 'Lecture IV: on Dryden and Pope', in *Lectures on English Poets*, London, 1924, pp. 104–29 (104–5, 120–1).

THOMAS BABINGTON MACAULAY: 1828

John Dryden

The public voice has assigned to Dryden the first place in the second rank of our poets,—no mean station in a table of intellectual precedency so rich in illustrious names. It is allowed that, even of the few who were his superiors in genius, none has exercised a more extensive or permanent influence on the national habits of thought and expression. His life was commensurate with the period during which a great revolution in the public taste was effected; and in that revolution he played the part of Cromwell. By unscrupulously taking the lead in its wildest excesses, he obtained the absolute guidance of it. By trampling on laws, he acquired the authority of a legislator. By signalizing himself as the most daring and irreverent of rebels, he raised himself to the dignity of a recognized prince. He commenced his career by the most frantic outrages. He terminated it in the repose of established sovereignty,—the author of a new code, the root of a new dynasty. . . .

Amidst the crowd of authors who, during the earlier years of Charles the Second, courted notoriety by every species of absurdity and affectation, he speedily became conspicuous. No man exercised so much influence on the age. The reason is obvious. On no man did the age exercise so much influence. He was perhaps the greatest of those whom we have designated as the critical poets; and his literary career exhibited, on a reduced scale, the whole history of the school to which he belonged,—the rudeness and extravagance of its infancy,—the propriety, the grace, the dignified good sense, the temperate splendour of its maturity. His imagination was torpid, till it was awakened by his judgement. He began with quaint parallels and empty mouthing. He gradually acquired the energy of the satirist, the gravity of the moralist, the rapture of the lyric poet. The revolution through which English literature has been passing, from the time of Cowley to that of Scott, may be seen in miniature within the compass of his volumes. . . .

He possessed, as we have said, in a pre-eminent degree, the power of reasoning in verse; and this power was now peculiarly useful to him. His logic is by no means uniformly sound. On points of criticism, he always reasons ingeniously; and, when he is disposed to be honest, correctly. But the theological and political questions which he undertook to treat in verse were precisely those which he understood least. His arguments, therefore, are often worthless. But the manner in which they are stated is beyond all praise. The style is transparent. The topics follow each other in the happiest order. The objections are drawn up in such a manner that the whole fire of the reply may be brought to bear on them. The circumlocutions which are substituted for technical phrases are clear, neat, and exact. The illustrations at once adorn and elucidate the reasoning. The sparkling epigrams of Cowley, and the simple garrulity of the burlesque poets of Italy, are alternately employed, in the happiest manner, to give effect to what is obvious, or clearness to what is obscure. . . .

His mind was of a slovenly character,—fond of splendour, but indifferent to neatness. Hence most of his writings exhibit the sluttish magnificence of a Russian noble, all vermin and diamonds, dirty linen and inestimable sables. Those faults which spring from affectation, time and thought in a great measure removed from his poems. But his carelessness he retained to the last. If towards the close of his life he less frequently went wrong from negligence, it was only because long habits of composition rendered it more easy to go right. In his best pieces we find false rhymes,—triplets, in which the third line appears to be a mere intruder, and, while it breaks the music, adds nothing to the meaning,—gigantic Alexandrines of fourteen and sixteen syllables, and truncated verses for which he never troubled himself to find a termination or a partner. . . .

The advantages which Dryden derived from the nature of his subject he improved to the very utmost. His manner is almost perfect. The style of Horace and Boileau is fit only for light subjects. The Frenchman did indeed attempt to turn the theological reasonings of the Provincial Letters into verse, but with very indifferent success. The glitter of Pope is cold. The ardour of Persius is without brilliancy. Magnificent versification and ingenious combinations rarely harmonize with the expression of deep feeling. In Juvenal and Dryden alone we have the sparkle and the heat together. . . .

He may, on the whole, be pronounced to have been a man possessed of splendid talents, which he often abused, and of a sound judgement, the admonitions of which he often neglected; a man who succeeded only in an inferior department of his art, but who, in that department, succeeded pre-eminently; and who with a more independent spirit, a more anxious desire of excellence, and more respect for himself, would, in his own walk, have attained to absolute perfection.

From *Works of Thomas Babington Macaulay*, Albany Edition, London, 1898, Vol. 7, pp. 114–66 (114, 143, 159, 162, 163, 166).

HIPPOLYTE TAINE: 1864

The Classic Age: Dryden

Under Spenser and Shakespeare, living words, like cries or music, betrayed the internal imagination which gave them forth. A kind of vision possessed the artist; landscapes and events were unfolded in his mind as in nature; he concentrated in a glance all the details and all the forces which make up a being, and this image acted and was developed within him like the external object; he imitated his characters; he heard their words; he found it easier to represent them with every pulsation than to relate or explain their feelings; he did not judge, he saw; he was an involuntary actor and mimic; drama was his natural work, because in it the characters speak, and not the author. Then this complex and imitative conception changes colour and is decomposed: man sees things no more at a glance, but in detail; he walks leisurely round them, turning his light upon all their parts in succession. The fire which revealed them by a single illumination is extinguished; he observes qualities, marks aspects, classifies groups of actions, judges and reasons. Words, before animated, and as it were swelling with sap, are withered and dried up; they become abstractions; they cease to produce in him figures and landscapes; they only set in motion the relics of enfeebled passions; they barely shed a few flickering beams on the uniform texture of his dulled conception; they become exact, almost scientific, like numbers, and like numbers they are arranged in a series, allied by their analogies,—the first, more simple, leading up to the next, more composite,—all in the same order, so that the mind which enters upon a track, finds it level, and is never obliged to quit it. Thenceforth a new career is opened; man has the whole world resubjected to his thought; the change in his thoughts has changed all aspects, and everything assumes a new form in his metamorphosed mind. His task is to explain and to prove; this, in short, is the classical style, and this is the style of Dryden.

He develops, defines, concludes; he declares his thought, then takes it up again, that his reader may receive it prepared, and having received, may retain it. He bounds it with exact terms justified by the dictionary, with simple constructions justified by grammar, that the reader may have at every step a method of verification and a source of clearness. He contrasts ideas with ideas, phrases with phrases, so that the reader, guided by the contrast, may not deviate from the route marked out for him. You may imagine the possible beauty of such a work. This poesy is but a stronger prose. Closer ideas, more marked contrasts, bolder images, only add weight to the argument. Metre and rhyme transform the judgements into sentences. The mind, held on the stretch by the rhythm, studies itself more, and by means of reflection arrives at a noble conclusion. The judgements are enshrined in abbreviative images, or symmetrical lines, which give them the solidity and popular form of a dogma. General truths acquire the definite form which transmits them to posterity, and propagates them in the human race. Such is the merit of these poems; they please by their good expressions. In a full and solid web stand out cleverly connected or sparkling threads. Here Dryden has gathered in one line a long argument; there a happy metaphor has opened up a new perspective under the principal idea; further on, two similar words, united together, have struck the mind with an unforeseen and cogent proof; elsewhere a hidden comparison has thrown a tinge of glory or shame on the person who least expected it. These are all artifices or successes of a calculated style, which chains the attention, and leaves the mind persuaded or convinced. . . .

Under his regular versification the artist's soul is brought to light; though contracted by habits of classical argument, though stiffened by controversy and polemics, though unable to create souls or to depict artless and delicate sentiments, he is a genuine poet: he is troubled, raised by beautiful sounds and forms; he writes boldly under the pressure of vehement ideas: he surrounds himself willingly with splendid images; he is moved by the buzzing of their swarms, the glitter of their splendours; he is, when he wishes it, a musician and a painter; he writes stirring airs, which shake all the senses, even if they do not sink deep into the heart.

From *The History of English Literature,* trans. H. Van Laun, 4 Vols, New York, 1889, Vol. 3, pp. 1–72 (59–61, 68–9).

MATTHEW ARNOLD: 1880

The Study of Poetry: Dryden and Pope

We are to regard Dryden as the puissant and glorious founder, Pope as the splendid high priest, of our age of prose and reason, of our excellent and indispensable eighteenth century. For the purposes of their mission and destiny their poetry, like their prose, is admirable. Do you ask me whether Dryden's verse, take it almost where you will, is not good?

A milk-white Hind, immortal and unchanged,
Fed on the lawns and in the forest ranged.

I answer: Admirable for the purposes of the inaugurator of an age of prose and reason. Do you ask me whether Pope's verse, take it almost where you will, is not good?

To Hounslow Heath I point, and Banstead Down;
Thence comes your mutton, and these chicks my own.

I answer: Admirable for the purposes of the high priest of an age of prose and reason. But do you ask me whether such verse proceeds from men with an adequate poetic criticism of life, from men whose criticism of life has a high seriousness, or even, without that high seriousness, has poetic largeness, freedom, insight, benignity? Do you ask me whether the application of ideas to life in the verse of these men, often a powerful application, no doubt, is a powerful *poetic* application? Do you ask me whether the poetry of these men has either the matter or the inseparable manner of such an adequate poetic criticism; whether it has the accent of

Absent thee from felicity awhile . . .

or of

And what is else not to be overcome . . .

or of

O martyr souded in virginitee!

I answer: It has not and cannot have them; it is the poetry of the builders of an age of prose and reason. Though they may write in verse, though they may in a certain sense be masters of the art of versification, Dryden and Pope are not classics of our poetry, they are classics of our prose.

From 'The Study of Poetry', *Essays in Criticism, Second Series* in *The Works of Matthew Arnold*, London, 1903, pp. 1–41 (30–1).

JAMES RUSSELL LOWELL: 1893

Dryden

It may be conceived that he was even painfully half-aware of having fallen upon a time incapable, not merely of a great poet, but perhaps of any poet at all; for nothing is so sensitive to the chill of a sceptical atmosphere as that enthusiasm which, if it be not genius, is at least the beautiful illusion that saves it from the baffling quibbles of self-con-sciousness. Thrice unhappy he who, born to see things as they might be, is schooled by circumstances to see them as people say they are,—to read God in a prose translation. Such was Dryden's lot, and such, for a good part of his days, it was by his own choice. He who was of a stature to snatch the torch of life that flashes from lifted hand to hand along the generations, over the heads of inferior men, chose rather to be a link-boy to the stews. . . .

Whatever else Dryden may have been, the last and abiding impression of him is, that he was thoroughly manly; and while it may be disputed whether he was a great poet, it may be said of him, as Wordsworth said of Burke, that 'he was by far the greatest man of his age, not only abounding in knowledge himself, but feeding, in various directions, his most able contemporaries'. . . .

Viewed from one side, he justifies Milton's remark of him, that 'he was a good rhymist, but no poet'. To look at all sides, and to distrust the verdict of a single mood, is, no doubt, the duty of a critic. But how if a certain side be so often presented as to thrust forward in the memory and disturb it in the effort to recall that total impression (for the office of a critic is not, though often so misunderstood, to say *guilty* or *not guilty* of some particular fact) which is the only safe ground of judge-ment? It is the weight of the whole man, not of one or the other limb of him, that we want. *Expende Hannibalem*. Very good, but not in a scale capacious only of a single quality at a time, for it is their union, and not their addition, that assures the value of each separately. It was not this or that which gave him his weight in council, his swiftness of decision in battle that outran the forethought of other men,—it was Hannibal. But this prosaic element in Dryden will force itself upon me. As I read him, I cannot help thinking of an ostrich, to be classed with flying things, and capable, what with leap and flap together, of leaving the earth for a longer or shorter space, but loving the open plain, where wing and foot help each other to something that is both flight and run at once. . . .

Was he, then, a great poet? Hardly, in the narrowest definition. But he was a strong thinker who sometimes carried common sense to a height where it catches the light of a diviner air, and warmed reason till it had wellnigh the illuminating property of intuition. Certainly he is not, like Spenser, the poets' poet, but other men have also their rights. Even the Philistine is a man and a brother, and is entirely right so far as he sees. To demand more of him is to be unreasonable. And he sees, among other things, that a man who undertakes to write should first have a meaning perfectly defined to himself, and then should be able to set it forth clearly in the best words. This is precisely Dryden's praise, and amid the rickety sentiment looming big through misty phrase which marks so much of modern literature, to read him is as bracing as a northwest wind. He blows the mind clear. In ripeness of mind and bluff heartiness of expression, he takes rank with the best. His phrase is always a short-cut to his sense, for his estate was too spacious for him to need that trick of winding the path of his thought about, and planting it out with clumps of epithet, by which the landscape-gardeners of litera-ture give to a paltry half-acre the air of a park. In poetry, to be next-best is, in one sense, to be nothing; and yet to be among the first in any kind of writing, as Dryden certainly was, is to be one of a very small com-pany. He had, beyond most, the gift of the right word. And if he does not, like one or two of the greater masters of song, stir our sympathies by that indefinable aroma so magical in arousing the subtile associations of the soul, he has this in common with the few great writers, that the winged seeds of his thought embed themselves in the memory and germinate there. If I could be guilty of the absurdity of recommending to a young man any author on whom to form his style, I should tell him that, next to having something that will not stay unsaid, he could find no safer guide than Dryden.

Cowper, in a letter to Mr Unwin (5th January, 1782), expresses what I think is the common feeling about Dryden, that, with all his defects, he had that indefinable something we call Genius. 'But I admire Dryden most [he had been speaking of Pope], who has succeeded by mere dint of genius, and in spite of a laziness and a carelessness almost peculiar to himself. His faults are numberless, and so are his beauties. His faults are those of a great man, and his beauties are such (at least sometimes) as Pope with all his touching and retouching could never equal.'

From *Among My Books*, Boston, 1893, pp. 1–80 (7, 8, 17, 78–80).

MARK VAN DOREN: 1920

The Poetry of John Dryden

The only qualities which Wordsworth could find in Dryden deserving to be called poetical were 'a certain ardour and impetuosity of mind' and 'an excellent ear'. Whether or not Wordsworth stopped short of justice in his enumeration, he hit upon two virtues which are cardinal in Dryden, and confined himself with proper prudence to what in Dryden is more important than any other thing, his manner. His manner, embracing both an enthusiastic approach to any work and a technical dexterity in the performance of it, was constant. The channels through which his enthusiasm drove him were not always fitted for his passage, as we have been seeing; nor was his ease of motion always an advantage, inasmuch as his metrical felicity served at times only to accentuate his original error in choice of province. But when his material was congenial, and when he himself was thoroughly at home in his style, he was unexceptionable.

Dryden was most at home when he was making statements. His poetry was the poetry of statement. At his best he wrote without figures, without transforming passion. When Shakespeare's imagination was kindled his page thronged with images. When Donne was most genuinely possessed by his theme he departed in a passionate search for conceits. When Dryden became fired he only wrote more plainly. The metal of his genius was silver, and the longer it was heated the more silver it grew. Nausicaa fell in love with Odysseus because the goddess Athene had shed a strange grace about his head and shoulders and made him seem more presentable than he was. No one can be impressed by Dryden who sees him in disguise. One must see him as he is: a poet of opinion, a poet of company, a poet of civilization. It is not to be inferred that he was without passion; but it is true that he never got outside himself. His passion was the passion of assurance. His great love was the love of speaking fully and with finality, his favourite subjects being persons and books. . . .

But let it be said again, the story of Dryden's conquest of English poetry for the most part is the story not of his material but of his manner. It is the story of a poet who inherited a medium, perfected it by long manipulation, stamped it with his genius, and handed it on. That medium was heroic couplet verse. . . .

Lowell notwithstanding, he is as much as Spenser a poet for poets. Not only in his own generation, or in the next, but in all that have succeeded he has stood on the shelves of writers and offered the stimulus of a style that is both musical and stout. Poets of widely varying complexions have made important use of him, never exactly reproducing him, for that is impossible even if desirable, but drawing from him the strength of the beauty they have seemed to need.

In the eighteenth century he shared with Milton and Pope the distinction, enviable or not, of inspiring the 'poetic diction' which Wordsworth later on was to receive so coldly. Milton in blank verse and Dryden and Pope in the heroic couplet were, if Spenser and his stanza be for the moment disregarded, the great models of versification under Queen Anne and the first two Georges. On the side of the heroic couplet Dryden exercised two varieties of influence according as he was identified with Pope or distinguished from him. In a certain sense he had identified himself with Pope when he had created him; for if Dryden had not written, it is a question what Pope would be. 'I learned versification wholly from Dryden's works', Pope told Spence; he has echoed Dryden everywhere, not only cadence for cadence but sometimes word for word and line for line. Zimri and Og begat Wharton and Sporus; *Mac Flecknoe* begat the *Dunciad*; the *Religio Laici* and *The Hind and the Panther* begat the *Moral Essays*; the *Cecilia* of 1687 begat the *Cecilia* of 1708; the *Virgil* begat the *Homer*; and the *Fables* begat the *Paraphrases from Chaucer*. Yet in another sense Pope derived not from Dryden at all, but from the smooth, equable tradition of Sandys and Waller. Poets who knew this, and who set Dryden's 'genius' over against Pope's correctness, thought to capture the secret of that 'genius'. In the first place, they remarked, Dryden, for an Augustan, was bewildering in his variety. . . . In the second place he was impetuous and, when need was, negligent. The negligence was easy to approximate, the impetuosity not so easy.

From Chapters 3 and 7 of *John Dryden: A Study of His Poetry*, Bloomington, Indiana, 1960, [originally published as *The Poetry of John Dryden*, New York, 1920], pp. 67–106 and 233–66 (67–8, 68–9, 258, 259).

Modern Critics on Dryden

EARL MINER: 1961

Dryden and the Issue of Human Progress

Recent studies of the intellectual history of the seventeenth century have added greatly to our knowledge of the writers and issues of the age. Of the major writers of the century, John Dryden perhaps remains darkest of all, even on such a crucial issue as his views concerning human progress.[1] In a way, the silence concerning Dryden is surprising, since he probably wrote more progress-pieces than any other of our poets.[2] But the silence is less perplexing when we consider the too seldom acknowledged difficulty of his poetry. With the scholarship so meagre and the difficulties so great, one can only take heart at the abundance of the evidence and attempt a brief and preliminary analysis of the

---

[1] A brief review of books will show how Dryden has been avoided. J. B. Bury quotes Dryden but once as a flourish to end a chapter in *The Idea of Progress*, New York, 1932, 1955. Victor Harris focuses upon the earlier part of the period in *All Coherence Gone*, Chicago, 1949, and leaves Dryden to the footnotes. Dryden is not even mentioned in: Ernest Tuveson, *Millenium and Utopia*, Berkeley, 1949; in R. U. Sampson, *Progress in the Age of Reason*, Cambridge, Mass., 1956; or in Michael Macklem, *The Anatomy of the World . . . from Donne to Pope*, Minneapolis, 1958. Only R. F. Jones comes to grips with Dryden on this issue in his *Ancients and Moderns*, St Louis, 1936, and in 'Science and Criticism in the Neo-Classical Age of English Literature', *JHI*, Vol. 1, 1940. Professor Jones has taken his evidence chiefly from the complex and sometimes ambiguous arguments in 'An Essay of Dramatic Poesy' and from other prose writings. My purpose is to infer Dryden's stand from his poetry; and although my conclusions sometimes differ from Professor Jones's, I wish to acknowledge the insights presented by him, as also by Louis I. Bredvold, *The Intellectual Milieu of John Dryden*, Ann Arbor, 1934, 1956.

[2] The chief progress-pieces in poetry and prose are: on knowledge in the poem to Dr Charleton; on commerce in the digression of 'Annus Mirabilis'; on poetic style in the Epilogue and Defense of the Epilogue to the second part of *The Conquest of Granada*; on arts and sciences in the poem to Roscommon; on music in the 'Song for St Cecilia's Day'; on English drama in the poem to Congreve; on painting in the poem to Kneller; on satire in the 'Discourse Concerning the Original and Progress of Satire'; and on the Restoration itself in *The Secular Masque*. His comments in isolated short passages defy listing.

poetry, hoping to elicit further study and to suggest, if possible, a useful critical approach.

Although they tend to avoid Dryden, historians of progress have shown that the issue posed four problems to the seventeenth century. There was a more or less continuous dispute whether perfection should be expected in a millenial convulsion or in an ordered advance brought about by human endeavour; and there were three successive although overlapping debates: whether nature is in decay since the Fall, whether the ancient or modern science is the superior, and whether the ancient or modern writers are to be preferred. Dryden's stand on these last three may be discussed first.

The controversy over the decay of nature had been settled by Dryden's time—there was scarcely a poet who any longer wrote of history in terms of post-lapsarian decay.[3] The debate over the ancient and modern science is another problem. Even professed 'Ancients' (such as Crites in the 'Essay of Dramatic Poesy' and Sir William Temple) believed in the superiority of modern science. But the question is rather one of the degree of enthusiasm, of the strength of faith in the promises of the new science. Professor Jones has convinced us that Dryden was a proponent of modern science, but the degree of his enthusiasm is a knotty problem. Even in his prose Defense of the 'Essay of Dramatic Poesy', he states that his method in the 'Essay' had been 'sceptical, according to that way of reasoning which was used by Socrates, Plato, and all the Academics of old, which Tully and the best of the Ancients followed, and which is imitated by the modest inquisitions of the Royal Society'.[4] Dryden can hardly be called a fervent supporter of the new science in the face of a declaration that its 'inquisitions' were so modest and imitative of five groups of Ancients. The really significant fact seems to be that in spite of his response to almost everything that moved him in his age, he wrote no Cowleyan ode on the Royal Society, as he surely would have, if he had placed his strongest hopes in the new science. His seemingly scientific curiosity was rather a sceptical turn of mind which was to take him, not into a society of perfected virtuosi, but into the Roman communion.

The third great debate over progress was the controversy over ancient and modern writers, but this issue is less important for Dryden than it may seem. The Battle of the Books did not become open warfare till the end of his life, and his sound critical sense saved him from taking any extreme position. A poet who could create perhaps more new literary forms than any other English writer and who argued that 'Our ladies and our men now speak more wit/In conversation' than the

[3] Milton is of course the great exception. As far as I know, Dryden makes affirmative use of the idea of decay only once—in the Epistle Dedicatory to the *Life of Plutarch*, Scott-Saintsbury, Vol. 17, pp. 5–6. But his purely rhetorical purpose there is evident from his use of a cyclical theory of history as well. And I hope to make clear in what follows that neither of these views was really held by Dryden.

[4] W. P. Ker, ed., *Essays of John Dryden*, Oxford, 1926, Vol. 1, p. 124.

Elizabethans 'writ' was no diehard ancient; and just as surely, the poet who had echoed Virgil, Ovid and Lucretius in his poems for decades and who enjoyed translating them was no radical modern either. His allegiance to the past was motivated by a desire to write literature in the present, and contrariwise he felt that there was small chance for a great modern literature which did not grow from a knowledge of the past. Such a moderate and sensible attitude makes the controversy seem irrelevant.

The three usual criteria for mustering writers on one side or the other in the debate over progress do not contribute very much to understanding of Dryden. (The question of 'millenium and utopia' will be dealt with later.) We must rather ask ourselves what his poems and, to a lesser extent, his critical writings tell us about his lifelong concern with progress. His awareness of change and his concern with progress seem to have meant two things: a sharpening of his critical sense from a heightened awareness of the relation of the past to the present and an inspiration for imagery and metaphor.

Some of Dryden's best recent critics have characterized his critical sensibility as one which thought in critical pairs which are sometimes antithetical and sometimes similar but differing. An example from the Defense of the Epilogue to the second part of *The Conquest of Granada* will illustrate this critical method of contrasts, springing into being under the stimulus of the progress theme. Dryden had been roundly berated for saying in the Epilogue that the Restoration had produced better poets than the Elizabethans; he protests he had not. Let us consider, he urges, the changes that have taken place in the wit, language, and the versification of our poetry. The change is obvious, but does it represent progress or regress? His analysis of *Sejanus* proves that it has been for the better, that progress has been made in refining wit, language, and versification. He does not argue that he and others have surpassed Jonson and Shakespeare in poetic genius; but genius is beyond any man's control, while refinement is not. His opposition of genius and refinement is a sensible one and one, moreover, that gives progress its due without becoming doctrinaire. Such sensible and sensitive judgement and an awareness of the issue of progress made it possible for him to treat literature for the first time in English criticism as a developing, living whole in which meaningful change is desired from age to age, but is not a determinant of the ultimate accomplishment of any one period.

Such matters are to be insisted upon if we are to understand such an out-and-out progress-piece as the witty and complex poem to Roscommon. The progress here is that of arts and knowledge, or of *translatio studii*, from the dawn of history to AD 1684 and into the future. The complex wit of the poem surrounds the meaning of 'translation': both rendering into another language—the kind of translation Roscommon had discussed in his 'Essay on Translated Verse'—and translation as transfer or progress.

Whether the fruitful Nile, or Tyrian shore,
The seeds of arts and infant science bore,
'Tis sure the noble plant, translated first,
Advanc'd its head in Grecian gardens nurs'd.
The Grecians added verse; their tuneful tongue
Made nature first and nature's God their song.
Nor stopp'd translation here; for conquering Rome
With Grecian spoils brought Grecian numbers home. (lines 1–8)

'Translation' continues: the middle ages add rhyme—'a kind of hob-
bling prose. . . . At best a pleasing sound, and fair barbarity'—to verse;
then rhymed poetry is improved by Dante and Petrarch, embellished
by the French, and given a 'manly sweetness' by the British. Is this
then an ironic progress-piece, accusing modern poets of debasing
poetry with rhyme? It seems to be, and in part it is, but after all we
see that Dryden has written his poem in rhyme—to the extent of using
four triplets in a short poem—and that his argument is directed toward
another point, his friend Roscommon:

The wit of Greece, the gravity of Rome,
Appear exalted in the British loom;
The Muses' empire is restor'd again,
In Charles his reign, and by Roscommon's pen. (lines 26–9)

Dryden's wit unites a pair of critical concepts—progress and linguistic
translation—in a double unity by calling them both translation and by
exemplifying them in the work of his friend Roscommon.

The witty double concept is continued and given a deeper meaning,
because progress-translation leads to another critical pair when Dryden
exclaims, 'How will translation and invention thrive' with Roscommon's
impetus! To simplify the logic somewhat, he holds that both judgement
(the faculty necessary for good rendering of the ancients) and imagina-
tion (the 'invention' of original poems) will increasingly thrive in an
England enlightened by Roscommon. This claim is extended further
through metaphor, since Homer and Virgil are to be brought, by some
means or other, into the stately palace of English poetry. They will
enter by translation, of course: by 'translation' as the natural progress
or development of Western culture and by 'translation' as an art
explained by Roscommon. But also through 'translation' by John
Dryden, since the last line of the poem is a Virgilian echo; for when
Dryden says of Homer and Virgil, that 'without stooping they may pass
the gate', we are meant to recall that Aeneas had to stoop to take himself
and Trojan culture into the palace of Evander. Virgil and Homer will,
however, pass undiminished into the palace of the Augustan age.
Progress is here the history of literary development and an inspiration
for literary criticism and Augustan literary ideals.

As the image of the Virgilian-English palace in 'Roscommon' shows, the idea of progress was a source of rich metaphors for Dryden. Some of the most common images that concern with progress inspired in his poetry are those of gardens and growth in such poems as those to Roscommon and Congreve; imagery of royal progress, whether the affirmative one of Virgil and Homer into Roscommon's palace of English poetry, or the ironic one of Shadwell and Flecknoe to their throne in the brothels near Barbican; and many other images. Two types of imagery emerge from his progress-pieces, I believe, and suggest his dual concept of progress. There are images of progress as process—growth or motion, and progress as an end achieved—the goal of art reached, for which he often employs imagery of stasis that is often architectural or transcendent.

Several of the ideas I have been suggesting cluster in a passage near the beginning of the poem to Congreve, where progress inspires literary criticism based upon distinctions employing such critical pairs as 'skill' and 'strength', cultivation or refinement and 'genius', and 'beauties' and 'strength'. At the same time, the progress-piece leads Dryden to employ imagery of growth and cultivation to describe the process or development of a literary tradition; and the result of progress is the architectural temple image signifying achievement.

Like Janus [Charles] the stubborn soil manur'd,
With rules of husbandry the rankness cur'd;
Tam'd us to manners, when the stage was rude;
And boist'rous English wit with art indued.
Our age was cultivated thus at length,
But what we gain'd in skill we lost in strength.
Our builders were with want of genius curst;
The second temple was not like the first:
Till you, the best Vitruvius, come at length;
Our beauties equal, but excel our strength.

Progress-as-process suggests development and growth and leads to art as accomplishment, art as the end of progress.

This idea of progress to achieved art or knowledge is fundamental to Dryden's thoughts on the subject. If his principal images in such poems were characteristically static, one would feel entitled to say he believed in fixed values opposed to change; and if the images conveyed action, that he believed in progress. As it is, his poems combine images of motion and stasis, of natural growth and perfected art, and of similar pairs with the resulting complexity in his attitude and ideas. While he nowhere supports mere change, he treats it as an inevitable force reflected in growth and human action and at the same time suggests the necessity of shaping it meaningfully. Progress must lead to achievement or it is undesirable change. In the literary sphere, change is natural and, if intelligently directed, desirable; but the really great works of art endure steadfast upon the pillars of eternity.

c

Progress also raised a question about the meaning of change in human history. He and his age were asked, in effect, whether progress in history was possible or whether change was to be feared. As Professor Tuveson and others have shown, three of the most dominant theories of history in the century were the older, orthodox idea of perfection coming about through God's intervention at the Day of Judgement; the concept of cycles of growth and decay; and the belief that man's own changes might lead in orderly progress to perfection. Dryden's view seems not to have been quite any of these; apparently he felt that a good deal of progress is possible and desirable in time, but that perfection will come only when eternity begins at the Day of Judgement. To show how he expressed this view and how it differs from the views of other writers of the time requires close attention to one of his most complex progress-pieces.

Professor Tuveson shows that writers like Burnet often tried to combine the apocalyptic views of the book of Revelation with the optimistic belief in progress brought about by human endeavour, often with very fanciful notions about what would happen in the 'last days'.[5] Dryden seems to hold to the apocalyptic view in the closing lines of 'A Song for St Cecilia's Day':

> So, when the last and dreadful hour
> This crumbling pageant shall devour,
> The Trumpet shall be heard on high,
> The dead shall live, the living die,
> And Music shall untune the sky.

Here as always, however, it is dangerous to quote Dryden out of context. The poem as a whole is a complex combination of progress-pieces made to serve duty as a musical history of the universe (and of course to do justice to the poem's occasion). Harmony, for which music is the aptest symbol, creates the earth out of a chaos of 'jarring atoms', brings the elements 'in order to their stations', and progresses finally to the creation of man. So much for that segment of eternity which existed prior to human history. According to the concluding lines, the Day of Judgement will reverse this progress by destroying the earth and will establish a new order of divine reality in which the second segment of eternity will supersede human history. But between the two divisions of this divine progress-piece, Dryden inserts a double progress-piece of events which take place in time and yet are intimately related to the central subject of harmony. Stanzas II and VII deal with the progress of musical instruments from Jubal's first, primitive 'corded shell' (taken from Biblical history), to Orpheus' lyre (taken from classical history), and to St Cecilia's invention, the organ (taken from modern history). As always in Dryden's progress-pieces, progress reaches an end, however, in an

---

[5] Ernest Tuveson, *Millenium and Utopia*, Berkeley, 1949, pp. 116 ff. *et passim*.

image, act, or event which transcends time and change; and so here the trumpet of doom is the final stage in the progress of musical instruments, its sounds making all human instruments irrelevant.[6]

The trumpet of doom also concludes a progress-piece on the human passions for, as Dryden exclaims in lines 16 and 24, 'What passion cannot Music raise and quell!' The progress from the martial passions aroused by the earthly trumpet and drum, to the amorous passions inspired by the flute, lute, and violins, and to the holy love inspired by the organ is a psychological progress-piece not unlike the temporal progress-piece and indeed may be regarded almost as part of it, since Jubal, Orpheus, and St Cecilia (who receives separate mention in each progression) arouse their hearers too. But Dryden had said that music could quell as well as raise the passions, and if we compare the two progress-pieces in the middle sections of this poem with Timotheus' impresario effects on Alexander in 'Alexander's Feast', it seems almost as if he has either foregone half his ability to show how feelings may fall with some kinds of music or forgot that he said that music also quells the passions. He knew what he was doing, of course, and so withheld the ability to quell human passions from human instruments in order to reserve it for the trumpet of doom. In this way, the last lines of the poem conclude both the divine and the earthly progress-pieces, while the subject, harmony, remains constant throughout. The structure of the poem is so carefully and complexly wrought that it is no mere wordplay to say that it is basically a musical development, as Dryden intended in calling his ode a 'Song', and as Handel proved in his masterful musical setting. The poem's complex structure, its subject-metaphor of music, and its interweaving of a double human progress into a two-stage divine progress-piece make proper assessment of Dryden's view of history in the poem extremely difficult. I have suggested that he treats eternity as limitless parentheses to human history; so that what the 'Song' adds to the other progress-pieces is the important concept, really a postulate of faith, that there is an ultimate religious realm which transcends man's accomplishments. The question that remains is how much he felt might be achieved by man before the trumpet should sound and the dead be raised.

Perhaps the most crucial aspect of the debate over progress was whether man might achieve perfection through the exercise of his reason. To find out Dryden's views on this subject is to discover his deepest-held attitude toward progress, and Professor Bredvold's insistence upon the importance of 'Religio Laici' points us our direction.

[6] It has been suggested to me that such conclusions as this are almost vatic and may therefore suggest that Dryden held a view of the poet as prophet. He certainly was conscious of the future as well as of the past, and it is noteworthy that his 'prophecies' usually come at the end of a poem or at least after he has established the values by which to judge the future securely. See the conclusions of such poems as 'MacFlecknoe', 'Absalom', the 'Roscommon', 'Song for St Cecilia's Day', the 'Killigrew', and the 'Purcell'.

Dim as the borrow'd beams of moon and stars
To lonely, weary, wand'ring travelers,
Is Reason to the soul; and, as on high
Those rolling fires discover but the sky,
Not light us here, so Reason's glimmering ray
Was lent, not to assure our doubtful way,
But guide us upward to a better day.
And as those nightly tapers disappear
When day's bright lord ascends our hemisphere;
So pale grows Reason at Religion's sight;
So dies, and so dissolves in supernatural light. (lines 1–11)

This passage employs the poetic method we have seen in other poems; it is a progress-piece, now a 'progress of the soul', to borrow a title from Donne. And like the other progress-pieces, this one uses an important pair of opposites and imagery of motion culminating, like the 'Song', in transcendence. The crucial pairing we have come to expect is, of course, that of Reason and Religion. Both terms of the pair are conveyed in imagery of contrasting forms of light. The light of Reason is as 'dim' and 'rolling' as the moon and stars to travellers who need a better light, the light of 'a better day' when the Sun-Christ dissolves the paltry rays of our flickering minds. The goal is union with God, as the succeeding lines help make clear, not a rationalistic New Jerusalem through experimental science. This 'humiliation of the reason' is not the whole story of the passage, however. These lines remain a progress-piece in this world as well as to the next, since Reason, however imperfect, may 'guide' us to the 'better day'. Dryden is so careful to insist upon the weakness of human reason that perhaps Professor Bredvold has missed his qualified affirmation of it. For this passage reveals an attitude like that in other poems: change is valuable when it is true progress toward a desired end, but the progress itself is less significant than the accomplishment to which it leads, an accomplishment which lies outside the temporal progression from which it has grown.

In other poems, Dryden treats change with the same discrimination and with the kinds of metaphors we have seen. Images of growth relate true progress to our experience of time and nature. When historical progress or development leads to true achievement, he conveys the accomplishment in architectural images like the palaces of Roscommon and Congreve or the transcendence of supernatural light in 'Religio Laici'. When change is a regress to chaos or a deterioration, the progress is ironic, as in 'MacFlecknoe', or the images change to those of jarring atoms and ill-defined lumps to designate the anarchism of the radical sectarians and Whigs in 'The Medall', 'Absalom', and elsewhere. For Dryden, each accomplishment must be viewed in the light of its age, and behind this relativism, as behind the determination whether change is true progress, lie certain more-or-less fixed standards of excellence. These standards may be works of art if he is concerned with literary progress, religious faith if he is concerned with religion, or principles fixed by experience in political history if his subject is political— standards, that is, which are the revealed products of time but which transcend it. Such a historical awareness does not produce great poetry of itself, and its lack does not doom literature to triviality. But when it makes historical literary criticism possible for the first time, when it is the spring of metaphor, structure, and wit, and when it adds something new to the English poetic tradition, then such a sensibility makes poetry into exciting and lasting art. If John Dryden the poet was kind to history as well as literature, history has bestowed upon him a uniquely appropriate wreath of its own in recording the fact that he combined at once the roles of poet laureate and historiographer royal.

From 'Dryden and the Issue of Human Progress', *Philological Quarterly*, Vol. 40, No. 1, 1961, pp. 120–9 (120–9).

Absalom and Achitophel

Religio Laici' served to present a kind of poetry and a method of imagery different in many respects from the prologues and epilogues; 'Religio Laici' is a middle kind of verse discourse lying between satire and praise. 'Absalom and Achitophel' (1681) is also a poem distinct in kind from those heretofore discussed, and although it is usually designated a satiric poem, it has affinities with both the satiric and the laudatory prologues and epilogues. Written to be read, not delivered from the stage, this poem is distinguished from the short pieces for the theatre by its length and narrative method, but from the point of view of imagery there are close connections. The translation of particular personages and particular sequences of events into the value order is one of the offices performed by imagery in this poem as it was in those pieces for the theatre. 'Absalom and Achitophel' is a notable and a complex instance of such a translation, containing both the satiric drive toward disvalue, and the complementary drive toward value.

Si Propiùs stes/Te Capiet Magis (If you stand closer, you will be more taken by it)—this motto, from Horace's *Ars Poetica*, Dryden affixed to 'Absalom and Achitophel'. The motto can be interpreted in several ways, but it seems certainly to point to the contemporary persons and events which are represented in the poem. From this point of view, the poem's Jewish history is a veil to be pierced so that the features of English history beneath the veil may be traced in detail. This is a necessary undertaking. The poem is involved with two histories, Jewish and English, and the persons and incidents of both must be known. The analogies that are implicit in the identities of the poem must be made explicit. Once the details have been recognized, however, the fact of the comparison should not be forgotten. The poem's implicit assertion is that one history is like another. This assertion is basically a valuative assertion of the sort that is present in the parallels of Plutarch's *Lives*, but the implicit nature of this assertion in Dryden's poem gives the matter another turn.

By being about two histories at once, 'Absalom and Achitophel' is about neither. Jewish history is modified to fit English history, and English history modified to fit Jewish history; as a result, the action of the poem is a *tertium quid*, removed from the specifications of both histories and, in an important sense, not history at all. For example:

He to his Brother gives Supreme Command;
To you a Legacy of Barren Land:

Perhaps th' old Harp, on which he thrums his Layes:
Or some dull *Hebrew* Ballad in your Praise.

(lines 437–40; I, 228K)

The reference to a brother is appropriate to Charles, rather than to
David; the harp and the ballad are more clearly appropriate to David
than to Charles. Or, to take another case, the Sanhedrin is employed
in the poem as a metaphor of Parliament, but the Sanhedrin does not
belong to the history of David's reign.

In his preface Dryden disclaimed the role of inventor and claimed
that of historian: 'Were I the Inventour, who am only the Historian . . .'
(I, 216K). This disclaimer, however, is merely part of the thin pretence
that the poem is sheer Jewish history based on Second Samuel. It is
a gesture of modesty over the designedly evident fact of the invention
exhibited in the combination of the two histories.[1] Moreover, the use
of Jewish history emphasizes the valuative aspect of the history that
is drawn from a sacred book. The whole Judaeo-Christian tradition
has operated to transmute the history of the Jews into a moral order.
By fastening a set of English persons and a sequence of English events
to a set of Jewish persons and a sequence of Jewish events, Dryden has
set English history in a moral order. The imagery of the poem extends
this moral order beyond what is supplied by Second Samuel; the
imagery is extended to embody the full moral order of Christian theo-
logy, and it is in terms of that moral order that a part of English history
is judged. The imagery creates the intersection of 'never and always'
with 'then and in England'.

The direction which the imagery of the poem takes in bringing to
bear the full Christian order is suggested in some of the statements in
Dryden's preface: 'But, since the most excellent Natures are always the
most easy; and, as being such, are the soonest perverted by ill Counsels,
especially when baited with Fame and Glory; 'tis no more a wonder
that he withstood not the temptations of *Achitophel*, than it was for
Adam, not to have resisted the two Devils: the Serpent and the Woman.
. . . Were I the Inventour . . . I shoud certainly conclude the Piece,
with the Reconcilement of *Absalom* to *David*. . . . I have not, so much as
an uncharitable Wish against *Achitophel*; but, am content to be Accus'd
of a good natur'd Errour; and, to hope with *Origen*, that the Devil

---

[1] Dryden, of course, was not the first to make the connection between Jewish
and English history. An anonymous Catholic poem, 'Naboth's Vineyard', had
appeared in 1679, and in 1680 an anonymous tract, *Absalom's Conspiracy, or The
Tragedy of Treason*, was published. In 'The Originality of "Absalom and
Achitophel"', *Modern Language Notes*, 46, 1931, pp. 211–18, R. F. Jones has
shown that the application of the life of King David to English political situa-
tions began early in the seventeenth century. Jones points out that Nathanael
Carpenter's *Achitophel, or the Picture of a Wicked Politician*, published in 1627,
attained a sixth edition by 1641. This work drew the character of Achitophel and
applied the portrait especially to Catholic figures involved in political intrigue,
but Achitophel soon became a byword for a wicked politician and was freely
employed, especially in sermons, by both Puritans and Royalists.

himself may, at last, be sav'd. . . . God is infinitely merciful; and his
Vicegerent is only not so, because he is not Infinite' (I, 216K). An
examination of passages from the poem will show that the imagery
takes up the themes of God and man, the devil and the fall, the tempta-
tion of Adam and the temptation of Christ; perhaps the most important
feature of the imagery is the superimposing of two themes in the David-
Absalom relationship; the theme of God and Adam, and the theme of
God, the Father, and His beloved Son, Christ.

The imagery of the poem at an early stage introduces faint sugges-
tions of David as God and of Absalom as Adam and of the events in
paradise:

> What e'r he did was done with so much ease,
> In him alone, 'twas Natural to please.
> His motions all accompanied with grace;
> And *Paradise* was open'd in his face.
> With secret Joy, indulgent *David* view'd
> His Youthfull Image in his Son renew'd:
> To all his wishes Nothing he deny'd,
> And made the Charming *Annabel* his Bride.
>
> (lines 27–34; I, 217K)[2]

It is worth noticing that the account of David given in the lines following
the passage quoted above continues to hover near the aspect of David as
God:

> Thus Prais'd, and Lov'd, the Noble Youth remain'd,
> While *David*, undisturb'd, in *Sion* raign'd.
>
> (lines 41–2; I, 218K)

Sion, of course, refers quite specifically to the hill upon which David's
royal palace was built, and the metonymy which takes Sion for the
whole of Israel is frequent in the Bible; Sion, however, is also frequently
applied to the heavenly city of God, a metaphoric application which it
shares with the name Jerusalem.

The imagery, in dealing with the stirrings of rebellion against
Israel's monarch, presses more insistently the duality of David as king
and as God, and it also subsumes the populace in Adam's rebellion:

> The *Jews*, a Headstrong, Moody, Murmuring race,
> As ever try'd th' extent and stretch of grace;
> God's pamper'd people whom, debauch'd with ease,
> No King could govern, nor no God could please;

---

[2] Line 30, with its mention of paradise, Dryden seems to have recalled in a
more detailed evocation of Eden in 'To Her Grace The Dutchess of Ormond':

Whose Face is Paradise, but fenc'd from Sin:
For God in either Eye has plac'd a Cherubin.

(lines 155–6; IV, 1467K)

(Gods they had tri'd of every shape and size
That God-smiths could produce, or Priests devise:)
These *Adam*-wits, too fortunately free,
Began to dream they wanted libertie.

.   .   .   .

Those very *Jewes*, who, at their very best,
Their Humour more than Loyalty exprest,
Now, wondred why, so long, they had obey'd
An Idoll Monarch which their hands had made:
Thought they might ruine him they could create;
Or melt him to that Golden Calf, a State.

                         (lines 45–52, 61–6; I, 218K)

In both of the above passages the imagery involves the political ruler
with the divine ruler, and involves rebellion against the earthly king
with idolatry; the first passage connects rebellion against the earthly
king with Adam's rebellion against a divine restraint. 'State', which is
the contemporary term for a polity distinct from a true monarchy, is
given the metaphor of religious idolatry and error, the golden calf.
The nature of the imagery here makes it seem possible that the reference
in a later passage is different from or additional to what a series of editors,
Sir Walter Scott, George R. Noyes, and James Kinsley, have suggested;
the lines in question are:

The *Jews* well know their power: e'r *Saul* they Chose,
God was their King, and God they durst Depose.

                         (lines 417–18; I, 227K)

Professor Noyes has the following note on the second line of the
couplet: 'Alluding to the Commonwealth "without a king", established
in 1649, which is compared to the condition of Israel under the Judges.
It was brought to an end by the creation of the Protectorate under
Cromwell ("*Saul*") in 1653.'[3] Professor Kinsley, in his edition, simply
cites a note by Scott which Noyes may well have been following. An
expression so forceful and unqualified as 'God was their King' may, of
course, be aimed at the political cant of the Commonwealth period,
but the direct mention of deposition in the latter half of the line suggests
an allusion to Charles I, the last ruler in the sacramental succession
before the interruption of that succession by the Commonwealth and
by the rule of Cromwell, the popularly chosen as opposed to the
divinely made ruler. In any case, the deposition of God refers to the
interruption of rule by divine right, an interruption which occurred at
the execution of Charles I and was merely affirmed in the choice of
Cromwell as Protector. It was this interruption of the succession that
made it possible for 'the *Jews*' to regard Charles II as 'An Idoll Monarch
which their hands had made'.

[3] George R. Noyes, ed., *The Poetical Works of John Dryden*, Cambridge
Ed., Boston, [1909, 1937] 1950, p. 960, note to line 418.

The stirrings of unrest against David (Charles II) are directly linked, by way of the imagery, with unrest in Eden fanned and directed by the Devil:

> But, when to Sin our byast Nature leans,
> The carefull Devil is still at hand with means;
> And providently Pimps for ill desires:
> The Good old Cause reviv'd, a Plot requires.
> Plots, true or false, are necessary things,
> To raise up Common-wealths, and ruin Kings.
>
> (lines 79–84; I, 219K)

At the level of particulars, the 'Good old Cause' that is being revived is the cause of the Commonwealth against Charles I,[4] and the Devil who is at hand with means is the Earl of Shaftesbury; in terms of imagery, the 'Good old Cause' is perhaps hinted to be Satan's rebellion against God, and the plot, the Hell-engendered design against man in Eden. At any rate, political unrest is here given the image of original sin encouraged and enabled by the Devil, and the ruin of Charles II corresponds to Satan's purposed discomfiture of his eternal enemy, God.

'Dryden', Professor Verrall remarks, 'was . . . profoundly original. The Biblical parallel is used *to admit the "heroic style"*.'[5] Imagery suggestive of *Paradise Lost* is consistently applied to those who have risen against the king or who are plotting a new uprising:

> Some had in Courts been Great, and thrown from thence,
> Like Feinds, were harden'd in Impenitence.
>
> (lines 144–5; I, 220K)

The crucial role of the imagery in passages such as this needs to be stressed. Take away the simile, and 'Courts', 'thrown', and 'Impenitence' bury themselves in historical events; the court of the English king dismisses certain disaffected persons, and away from the court their disaffection hardens. The identification of English with Jewish history, of course, prevents this sheer particularism; what might otherwise be merely local is raised a notch to a generalization within history: 'Disaffected persons become fixed in their disloyalty away from court.' Only with the simile, 'like Feinds', does the full force of 'Impenitence' come into operation; with this image, 'Courts' takes on a bright lustre which carries over to 'thence', so that 'thrown from thence' has a pinnacle of reference from which the fall is epic, Satan's and Vulcan's,

---

[4] Professor Noyes' note on the passage gives the following explanation: '*Good Old Cause*. That is, of the Commonwealth; Dryden's aim is to identify the Whigs with the men who rebelled against Charles I. There is, possibly, a more specific reference to the intrigues between Charles I and the Presbyterians and the parliament in 1647–8, which led ultimately to the execution of the king and the establishment of the Commonwealth' (p. 958, note to line 82).

[5] *Lectures on Dryden*, Cambridge, 1914, p. 57.

the full enlargement of the Miltonic context with the impenitence hardened in Hell. It is the image, 'like Feinds', that refers history to judgement, 'never and always'.

The portrait of Achitophel which follows in lines 150–203 has been much admired, especially because it holds a residue of qualification and fairness that largely overcomes the stigma of mere faction. Achitophel is represented as sagacious, bold, a fiery soul, a great wit, blessed with wealth and honour; he is praised especially as a judge with discerning eyes and clean hands, ready without the stimulus of bribery or special pleading to redress the grievances of the wretched, 'Swift of Dispatch, and easie of Access'. The fairness of the portrait lies in the presentation of all sides of a many-sided man and in a willingness to recognize the role of contingency in shaping Achitophel's actions. The mitigations of the portrait are the mitigations possible with respect to a person of high qualifications in any particular historical situation. The portrait, however, also wears another and sterner aspect; among all the qualifications and mitigations there is steadily present the aspect of judgement, and the full verdict of that judgement appears in the imagery applied to Achitophel in this passage and in later sections of the poem.

The imagery of the portrait sets the mitigations in a different light by pressing down upon Achitophel the image of Satan, another figure of high qualifications and mitigated in his evil nature by some remnant glories:

> he above the rest
> In shape and gesture proudly eminent
> Stood like a Towr; his form had yet not lost
> All her Original brightness, nor appear'd
> Less then Arch Angel ruind . . .
>
> .   .   .   .
>
> Dark'n'd so, yet shon
> Above them all th' Arch Angel.[6]

The opening lines of the portrait are blunt enough, so blunt that the unstressed metaphor of the second line is easily missed:

> Of these the false *Achitophel* was first:
> A Name to all succeeding Ages Curst.
>
> (lines 150–1; I, 220–1K)

The name that is cursed for all succeeding ages is Achitophel, but it is not only Achitophel. More light is shed on the full identity of Achitophel later in the portrait in lines such as these:

> In Friendship False, Implacable in Hate:
> Resolv'd to Ruine or to Rule the State.

---

[6] *Paradise Lost*, I, lines 589–93, 599–600; quotations from Milton are from H. C. Beeching, ed., *The Poetical Works of John Milton*, Oxford, 1935.

> To Compass this the Triple Bond he broke; ⎫
> The Pillars of the publick Safety shook: ⎬
> And fitted *Israel* for a Foreign Yoke. ⎭
>
> (lines 173-7; I, 221K)

'Implacable in Hate' echoes the defiance of Milton's Satan pledging 'study of revenge, immortal hate' (*Paradise Lost*, I, line 107). The resolution to rule or ruin is a close reflection of the Satanic determination expressed in Beelzebub's address setting forth the project against God's creation:

> either with Hell fire
> To waste his whole Creation, or possess
> All as our own. . . .
>
> (*Paradise Lost*, II, lines 364-6)

And though the next three lines return as unmistakably to history (both Second Samuel and Restoration England), it is still a history with reverberations. The breaking of 'the Triple Bond', referring at the level of then and in England to the triple alliance formed in 1668 among England, Sweden, and the Dutch Republic against France, an alliance which Shaftesbury played a prominent part in breaking up, parallels on another level the action that Satan had to undertake to carry out his design against mankind:

> at last appeer
> Hell bounds high reaching to the horrid Roof,
> And thrice threefold the Gates; three folds were Brass,
> Three Iron, three of Adamantine Rock,
> Impenitrable. . . .
>
> (*Paradise Lost*, II, lines 643-7)

Likewise, across the description of Achitophel's son, reflecting historically the contempt in which he was held and Plato's definition of man (*implumis bipes*), flits perhaps the shadow of Milton's Chaos, and of another son:

> And all to leave, what with his Toyl he won,
> To that unfeather'd, two Leg'd thing, a Son:
> Got, while his Soul did hudled Notions try;
> And born a shapeless Lump, like Anarchy.
>
> (lines 169-72; I, 221K)
>
> The other shape,
> If shape it might be call'd that shape had none
> Distinguishable in member, joynt, or limb.
>
> (*Paradise Lost*, II, lines 666-8)[7]

---

[7] Professor Morris Freedman's article, 'Dryden's Miniature Epic', *Journal of English and Germanic Philology*, Vol. 57, 1958, pp. 211-19, argues for the probable functional allusion to *Paradise Lost* here and in other instances I have cited. Only in a minority of cases does my interpretation of the function of these allusions diverge from his.

And there is a further suggestion of Satan and a strong suggestion of Eden in the final lines:

Oh, had he been content to serve the Crown,
With vertues only proper to the Gown;
Or, had the rankness of the Soyl been freed
From Cockle, that opprest the Noble seed:
David, for him his tunefull Harp had strung,
And Heaven had wanted one Immortal song.
But wilde Ambition loves to slide, not stand;
And Fortunes Ice prefers to Vertues Land:
Achitophel, grown weary to possess
A lawfull Fame, and lazy Happiness;
Disdain'd the Golden fruit to gather free,
And lent the Croud his Arm to shake the Tree.

(lines 192–203; I, 222K)

Whatever weight we may be willing to give to any of these allusions individually, it is difficult not to feel that collectively they fill the portrait in: the 'Name to all succeeding Ages Curst' is '*Satan*', and the action which the imagery has gradually supplied to the portrait is the action of Satan's emergence from Hell for his attempt upon Eden. With all its mitigations, all its fairness at the level of representation of a gifted man, the judgement that the portrait holds over its subject is that he is the intrepid Devil himself emerging from Hell to destroy Eden and to devote man to death.

Dr Johnson found fault with the lapses in what he seems to have regarded as a simple parallelism of two histories: 'The original structure of the poem was defective: allegories drawn to great length will always break; Charles could not run continually parallel with David.'[8] The poem, however, as has been suggested earlier, is neither Jewish history nor English history but a *tertium quid*, an action somewhere between or above both histories and commenting on both. The imagery is *relevant* to both histories, but the images are designed and made *appropriate* in terms of the *tertium quid*, the fundamental action of the poem. There are instances where particulars of English history are related to particulars of Jewish history without resort to imagery; in these cases the action of the poem is simply not given a symbolic embodiment. The symbolic embodiment, the action in the imagery, rises above and dominates the whole mass of the particulars of both histories, but without appearing concretely in significant relation to each particular as it occurs. An occasional connection between Jewish history and English history with no image of God or Satan or Eden or Hell or Heaven can be accepted because the multiplicity of such connections *accompanied by* such images adequately establishes the general symbolic action; in the same way, a connection that specifically involves one but not both histories

[8] G. B. Hill, ed., *Lives of the Poets*, 3 Vols, Oxford, 1905, Vol. 1, pp. 436–7.

with the symbolic pattern can be accepted because the multiplicity of triple connections has adequately related both histories to the general symbolic action. In cases of the former type, historical parallels are prominent and the symbolic action distant; in cases of the latter type, the symbolic action is dominant. The former is more occupied with history and the latter more with value. The office performed by the imagery, as has been said earlier, is to provide an emblem of and residence for value.

The section of the poem which follows the portrait of Achitophel has been generally referred to by critics as 'The Temptation of Absalom'. In this section the imagery presents two major themes in combination, or superimposed upon one another: the theme of the temptation in the Garden and the theme of the temptation of Christ. The connection which the imagery makes between Absalom's and Adam's rebellion has already been pointed out as a suggestion in a passage of Dryden's preface and in several passages of the poem. In the section of the poem now to be considered, the Absalom-Adam relation is made unmistakable with the setting of the temptation partly in the context of the Garden; the imagery applied to Achitophel is the imagery of Satan as he appeared in the Garden, the arguments employed by Achitophel are a blend of Satan's arguments in the Garden and his arguments to Christ in the desert, and—the most important consideration—the event of the temptation is a fall. The Absalom-Christ relation is pressed by the images of Saviour and Messiah applied to Absalom, and by the main theme of the temptation, power over one of the kingdoms of this world.

In Achitophel's first address to Absalom, the tempter is associated with an aspect of the Garden and Absalom is given the images of the Messiah:

> Him [Absalom] he attempts, with studied Arts to please,
> And sheds his Venome, in such words as these.
>   Auspicious Prince! at whose Nativity
> Some Royal Planet rul'd the Southern sky;
> Thy longing Countries Darling and Desire;
> Their cloudy Pillar, and their guardian Fire:
> Their second *Moses*, whose extended Wand
> Divides the Seas, and shews the promis'd Land:
> Whose dawning Day, in every distant age,
> Has exercis'd the Sacred Prophets rage:
> The Peoples Prayer, the glad Deviners Theam,
> The Young-mens Vision, and the Old mens Dream!
> Thee, *Saviour*, Thee, the Nations Vows confess;
> And, never satisfi'd with seeing, bless.
>
> (lines 228–41; I, 223K)[9]

[9] Line 239 is an echo of the beginning of the apocalyptic section of Joel (2:28) which has sometimes been regarded as foreshadowing a Messianic kingdom.

It should be noticed, moreover, that Achitophel's argument occasionally adopts the form of Satan's argument in *Paradise Regained*. The following passage is part of Achitophel's argument:

> Our Fortune rolls, as from a smooth Descent,
> And, from the first Impression, takes the Bent:
> But, if unseiz'd, she glides away like wind;
> And leaves repenting Folly far behind.
> Now, now she meets you, with a glorious prize,
> And spreads her Locks before her as she flies.
> Had thus Old *David*, from whose Loyns you spring,
> Not dar'd, when Fortune call'd him, to be King,
> At *Gath* an Exile he might still remain,
> And heavens Anointing Oyle had been in vain.
>
> (lines 256–65; I, 223K)

The following lines are a part of Satan's argument in Book III of *Paradise Regained*:

> thy Kingdom though foretold
> By Prophet or by Angel, unless thou
> Endeavour, as thy Father *David* did,
> Thou never shalt obtain; prediction still
> In all things, and all men, supposes means,
> Without means us'd, what it predicts revokes.[10]
>
> (III, lines 351–56)

The Messianic token, Davidic lineage, appears as an authorizing phrase and as the Devil's flattery in both passages. Absalom's reply to Achitophel's first approach may be compared with part of Christ's reply to Satan in *Paradise Regained*. Absalom says:

> My Father Governs with unquestion'd Right;
> The Faiths Defender, and Mankinds Delight:
> Good, Gracious, Just, observant of the Laws;
> And Heav'n by Wonders has Espous'd his Cause.
> Whom has he Wrong'd in all his Peaceful Reign?
> Who sues for Justice to his Throne in Vain?
> What Millions has he Pardon'd of his Foes,
> Whom Just Revenge did to his Wrath expose?
> Mild, Easy, Humble, Studious of our Good;
> Enclin'd to Mercy, and averse from Blood.[11]
>
> (lines 317–26; I, 225K)

[10] Professor A. B. Chambers' note, 'Absalom and Achitophel: Christ and Satan', *Modern Language Notes*, 74, 1959, pp. 592–6, calls attention to the relevance of *Paradise Regained* to Dryden's handling of the temptation scene and suggests something of the dual Adam-Christ role of Absalom.

[11] 'Mankinds Delight', in the second line of this passage, is referred by Professor Noyes (p. 960) to Suetonius' *amor ac deliciae generis humani* applied to the Emperor Titus. Perhaps the phrase may also be referred to the psalmist's injunctions to delight in the Lord, Psalms 1:2 and 37:4; see also Job 34:9 and Isaiah 58:14.

Christ retorts to Satan's objection of the glory required by God of men:

> And reason; since his word all things produc'd,
> Though chiefly not for glory as prime end,
> But to shew forth his goodness, and impart
> His good communicable to every soul
> Freely; of whom what could he less expect
> Then glory and benediction, that is thanks,
> The slightest, easiest, readiest recompence
> From them who could return him nothing else,
> And not returning that would likeliest render
> Contempt instead, dishonour, obloquy?
>
> (*Paradise Regained*, III, lines 122–31)

These passages from *Paradise Regained* are not cited in an attempt to establish verbal parallels. They are cited simply to show that the identities suggested in the imagery of the poem, Satan for Achitophel and Christ for Absalom, are supported by the similarity in the arguments and sentiments expressed by Satan and Achitophel, Absalom and Christ. The significant difference between Absalom and Christ is that Absalom is the Messiah primarily in the mouth of Achitophel and of the people, a false Christ set up by Satan and accepted by the deceived populace, whereas Christ, rejected of men, is indeed the Son of God. At a later point in the poem, popular acceptance of Absalom as the Messiah is emphasized:

> The Croud, (that still believe their Kings oppress)
> With lifted hands their young *Messiah* bless.
>
> (lines 727–8; I, 235K)

The Messianic and Satanic imagery is, indeed, quite unmistakable in the poem. It is worth remarking that even Achitophel uses Satanic imagery; making brazenness do the work of guile, he applies Satanic imagery to David:

> He is not now, as when on *Jordan's* Sand
> The Joyfull People throng'd to see him Land,
> Cov'ring the *Beach*, and blackning all the *Strand*:
> But, like the Prince of Angels from his height,
> Comes tumbling downward with diminish'd light.
>
> (lines 270–4; I, 224K)

In this fashion Achitophel compounds falsehood and deception, creating false images both of the Messiah and of Satan, false pictures of both good and evil. In yielding to the temptation of Achitophel, in being deceived, Absalom shows that he is not the true son; he reverts to the status of Adam whose fall put an end to man's residence in Eden.

Absalom weakens and Achitophel triumphs; the imagery is primarily of the Garden:

> Why am I Scanted by a Niggard Birth?
> My Soul Disclaims the Kindred of her Earth:
> And made for Empire, Whispers me within;
> Desire of Greatness is a Godlike Sin.
>   Him Staggering so when Hells dire Agent found,
> While fainting Vertue scarce maintain'd her Ground,
> He pours fresh Forces in, and thus Replies:
>   Th' Eternal God Supreamly Good and Wise,
> Imparts not these Prodigious Gifts in vain;
> What Wonders are Reserv'd to bless your Reign?[12]
>
> (lines 369–78; I, 226K)

The special merit of the imagery is its functional character. The imagery points, on the one hand, to an Absalom (Adam) too much taken with his half-claim to royalty (a god-like nature) and desiring to be king (as a god), and, on the other hand, to an Achitophel playing upon Absalom's half-claim and desire by addressing him as the true son (Christ) and promising him dominion over one of the kingdoms of this world. The duality in the imagery applied to Absalom is impressive because it embodies the fact of his nature (man) and the nature of his temptation (to be more). His salvation lies in obedience and is the dear hope of David (as Monmouth's restoration to dutifulness was of Charles)—an earned sonship, a true sonship, is available to him. The epic accent introduced by the imagery lends to Absalom's choice the significance of Adam's.

Apart from the imagery employed in the portrait of Achitophel and the temptation of Absalom, there is a liberal sprinkling of anti-God imagery throughout the poem. The metaphor of David, God's anointed king, conditions the use of anti-God imagery for David's enemies; David himself characterizes his enemies in anti-God terms in his speech from the throne:

> Their *Belial* with their *Belzebub* will fight.
>
> (line 1016; I, 243K)

Shimei, one of the enemies of David, is represented as fostering anti-God forces:

> During his [Shimei's] Office, Treason was no Crime.
> The Sons of *Belial* had a glorious Time.
>
> (lines 597–8; I, 232K)

---

[12] Professor Verrall noticed the Miltonic context invoked in these lines and pointed to the Miltonic inversion in line 373 ('Him Staggering so when Hells dire Agent found') as a clear suggestion of Milton's Satan—*Lectures on Dryden*, p. 55.

D

The extension of the anti-God imagery to include anti-Christ imagery is conditioned by the fundamental departure from the Second Samuel context which is involved in the Messianic imagery. The Messianic imagery is within the Old Testament frame, but verges upon the actual New Testament Messiah (and the Christ of *Paradise Regained*). The anti-Christ imagery introduces New Testament contexts. There are, for example, suggestions of the Pharisees as the New Testament represents them in the portrait of Shimei:

> *Shimei*, whose Youth did early Promise bring
> Of Zeal to God, and Hatred to his King;
> Did wisely from Expensive Sins refrain,
> And never broke the Sabbath, but for Gain.
>
> (lines 585–8; I, 232K)

The New Testament context is unmistakably employed to create an anti-Christ portrait by skilful parody:

> For *Shimei*, though not prodigal of pelf,
> Yet lov'd his wicked Neighbour as himself:
> When two or three were gather'd to declaim ⎫
> Against the Monarch of *Jerusalem*,   ⎬
> *Shimei* was always in the midst of them.   ⎭
> And, if they Curst the King when he was by,
> Woud rather Curse, than break good Company.
>
> (lines 599–605; I, 232K)

The blasphemy of Shimei's coupled piety and acquisitiveness is effectively conveyed by a series of turns upon the language of various New Testament passages (notably Matthew 22:39 and 18:20) which artfully image the perversion.

The anti-God and anti-Christ forces have their stronghold in Jerusalem (London):

> But he [Jonas], tho bad, is follow'd by a worse,
> The wretch, who Heavens Annointed dar'd to Curse.
>
> .   .   .   .
>
> The City, to reward his [Shimei's] pious Hate
> Against his Master, chose him Magistrate.
>
> (lines 583–4, 593–4; I, 232K)

The populace, having tried 'Gods . . . of every shape and size', unsteady, fickle, 'humourous' rather than loyal, are represented as governed by the moon, and the imagery develops this emblem as a *leitmotiv* of the crowd, varying it in the related images of ebbing and flowing tides and pressing the lunar implications of inconstancy and madness:

> For, govern'd by the *Moon*, the giddy *Jews*
> Tread the same track when she the Prime renews:

And once in twenty Years, their Scribes Record,
By natural Instinct they change their Lord.

                                    (lines 216–19; I, 222K)

What Standard is there in a fickle rout,
Which, flowing to the mark, runs faster out?
Nor only Crowds, but Sanhedrins may be
Infected with this publick Lunacy.

                                    (lines 785–8; I, 237K)

The final section of the poem swings from Jerusalem and David's
opposition to the stalwart few who have bulwarked the throne, and to
David himself speaking from the throne. The movement is from satire
to praise, and, in the landscape of England, from London to Oxford.
Dr Johnson criticized adversely the concluding section of 'Absalom
and Achitophel'; his objection runs as follows: 'As an approach to
historical truth was necessary the action and catastrophe were not in
the poet's power; there is therefore an unpleasing disproportion between
the beginning and the end. We are alarmed by a faction formed out of
many sects various in their principles, but agreeing in their purpose of
mischief, formidable for their numbers, and strong by their supports,
while the king's friends are few and weak. The chiefs on either part are
set forth to view; but when expectation is at the height the king makes a
speech, and "Henceforth a series of new times began". Who can forbear
to think of an enchanted castle, with a wide moat and lofty battlements,
walls of marble and gates of brass, which vanishes at once into air when
the destined knight blows his horn before it?'[13] Dr Johnson admits that
what affects him as a 'disproportion between the beginning and the
end' was in some sort thrust upon Dryden by the historical facts.
Charles II's carefully managed surprise dissolution of the Oxford
Parliament had set the opposition members clamouring for horses and
scurrying out of Tory Oxford. The King's opposition was discomfited
and scattered quite as if the destined knight had blown his horn. There
is, moreover, beyond the historical facts, a consideration of some
weight that rests upon the action in the imagery of the poem. The sym-
bolic identity of the destined knight needs to be appreciated:

With all these loads of Injuries opprest,
And long revolving, in his carefull Breast,
Th' event of things; at last his patience tir'd,
Thus from his Royal Throne by Heav'n inspir'd,
The God-like *David* spoke: with awfull fear
His Train their Maker in their Master hear.
    Thus long have I, by native mercy sway'd,
My wrongs dissembl'd, my revenge delay'd:

. . . .

---

[13] *Lives of the Poets*, Vol. 1, p. 437. Dryden has 'time', not 'times' as quoted by
Dr Johnson.

Must I at length the Sword of Justice draw?
Oh curst Effects of necessary Law!
How ill my Fear they by my Mercy scan,
Beware the Fury of a Patient Man.
Law they require, let Law then shew her Face;
They coud not be content to look on Grace,
Her hinder parts, but with a daring Eye
To tempt the terror of her Front, and Dye.

.   .   .   .

Their *Belial* with their *Belzebub* will fight;
Thus on my Foes, my Foes shall do me Right:

.   .   .   .

Henceforth a Series of new time began,
The mighty Years in long Procession ran:
Once more the Godlike *David* was Restor'd,
And willing Nations knew their Lawfull Lord.[14]

(lines 933–40, 1002–9, 1016–17, 1028–31; I, 241–3K)

The symbolic matrix in which David is stoutly set for this final speech is clearly that of the acts and utterances of God. The context that may be invoked is the sixth book of *Paradise Lost* where God, after the indeterminacy of the struggle between his angels and Satan's host, on the third day takes effective action through his Son. The ease with which the rout of Satan's army is then accomplished is well known. Dr Johnson's comment needs to be considered in relation to this symbolic action. His estimate of the opposition is just: 'a faction formed out of many sects . . . agreeing in their purpose of mischief, formidable for their numbers, and strong by their supports'. Dr Johnson, however, underestimates the king; he speaks only of his supports: 'the king's friends are few and weak'.[15] The imagery enforces the consideration that symbolically this is the very King for whom gates of brass lift up their heads and bars of iron yield. In terms of the action in the imagery, 'the destined knight' who appears as a *deus ex machina* is the very God. The imagery, therefore, makes the balance between the King and his enemies more equal and calls in question what Dr Johnson termed the 'unpleasing disproportion between the beginning and the end'. The critical problem that arises has an affinity with that posed by the Saviour's single-handed defeat of Satan and his host in *Paradise Lost*. The remarkable and perhaps aesthetically improbable fact of Charles

---

[14] Professor Noyes' note on lines 1006 ff. (p. 963) is pertinent: 'Moses on Mount Sinai was not allowed to behold the face of the Lord, "For there shall no man see me, and live", he was permitted, however, to see the "back parts" of the Lord (Exodus 33: 20–3). Dryden here terms Grace the 'hinder parts' of Law: the Whigs have clamoured for Law against the Catholics and denied the king's power to grant pardon; hence they shall behold the face of Law and die themselves.'

[15] *Lives of the Poets*, Vol. 1, p. 437.

II's victory is made akin to God's victory over Satan; the imagery works to translate an unlikely historical event into value terms and thereby to lay hold on a greater aesthetic probability.

The action embodied in the imagery of 'Absalom and Achitophel' turns upon the basic metaphor of the Garden, Eden, for the kingdom. Shakespeare, for one, had employed this metaphor for the kingdom and, in *Richard II*, devoted a full scene (Act III, scene iv) to the symbolic consideration of the king as gardener. Gaunt, in his famous speech (Act II, scene i) speaks of England as 'This other Eden, demi-Paradise'. In the local condition of Denmark, Hamlet sees the state of the world and exclaims, "'Tis an unweeded garden' (Act I, scene ii). In Dryden's poem the kingdom is a paradise that may be lost and that may be regained. As it is man's—that is to say, as it is Charles II's and David's, Monmouth's and Absalom's, as it is Adam's—it is subject to loss; as the Garden is God's and man's and Satan is in it, the Garden hovers between being lost by man's action or saved by God's action. The evil attempt upon the Garden is at the centre of the poem. The historical personages, the human beings at the base of the action, give the metaphor of Adam a pervasive validity; there is an Adam assimilated to Satan in Achitophel, an Adam who falls in Absalom, and an unfallen Adam presiding over the Garden in David. On the other hand, the imagery of the Messiah that Achitophel applies to Absalom, false and guileful as the application is, points to an identity that, in the realm of value, is potential in the true son of David, and points beyond that to the identity potential in his father, David, the Maker in the master.

'Absalom and Achitophel' is a complex poem. The variety of its elements is not satisfactorily contained under the tent of satire, and there is a good deal to be said for Professor Verrall's suggestion that the poem be classified as an '*epyllion*, or epic in miniature, comprising satiric elements'.[16] Such a classification can more easily assimilate the main facts about the poem which the present study of its imagery suggests: the presence of an epic action adumbrated in considerable detail by imagery in the heroic style, and the presence together in one poem of a focus of satire in London (the populace stirred up by Achitophel and Absalom) and a focus of praise in the king (David's speech from the throne fortified by the historical event of Charles II's speech at Oxford); both images of the king are here, the image of the king threatened and long-suffering and the image of the king asserting his power and triumphant. The difficulty which Dr Johnson found in reconciling the strength of the king's enemies with the king's sudden overpowering success is not quite resolved by considering it at the level of imagery, but translated to this level of the poem, Johnson's objection sheds new light. The phase of the epic action adumbrated in the London section of the poem is truncated; there is a Fall, but the consequences to Adam

[16] *Lectures on Dryden*, p. 59.

and to Eden are suspended. At the point of truncation a second phase of the epic action is adumbrated, the rout of Satan and his hosts by God. It may be that Dryden should be censured for cramming the frame of an 'epic in miniature' with two phases of an epic action which, in their new context and arrangement, will not submit to a neat joint. It may also be that such a critical demand misconceives the nature of a miniature epic; such a form must shrink or truncate the epic action, and it seems to have been Dryden's strategy, as the imagery suggests, to present certain epic panels, the parts of one large painting conveying the significant moments of an action, not the full continuity of the action.[17] In the first line of the poem there is a suggestion of romance epic, a suggestion of the fabulous: 'In pious times, e'r Priest-craft did begin.' Dr Johnson caught this same suggestion when he described the king as appearing at the end like the destined knight at the blast of whose horn the enchanted castle vanishes into air. It is really a very old aesthetic problem; the king threatened or deposed is credible, the king enthroned and ideal appears fabulous. 'Fled is that music:—Do I wake or sleep?'—London and our world always seem real; Oxford and Eden (and the nightingale) seem myths.

From Chapter 4 of *John Dryden's Imagery*, Gainesville, Florida, 1962, pp. 72–91 (72–91).

[17] Ruth Wallerstein has suggested that both 'Mac Flecknoe' and 'Absalom and Achitophel' have a kind of parallel in Renaissance painting, particularly in the Triumph paintings and in such group portraits as Lucas Cranach's 'Woman Taken in Adultery' where the construction is simple and where the portraits present typical attitudes—'To Madness Near Allied: Shaftesbury and His Place in the Design and Thought of "Absalom and Achitophel",' *Huntington Library Quarterly*, 6, 1943, p. 448.

Analogies for Poetry

Drilled as we are in poetic ambiguity and ambivalence, we are usually ready to applaud a writer's ability to synthesize the two halves of a comparison. I. A. Richards's distinction between tenor and vehicle, between the object, quality, or situation to be described by comparison with something else and the something else with which it is compared, has prompted critics to enquire into the way in which poetry frequently seems to break down the distinction.

In the figures used to illustrate normal discourse the vehicle or means of comparison remains subordinate to the tenor, the object or end of comparison. The simile, 'her hair's as black as coal', is accepted as a slightly more vivid superlative than 'her hair is very black'. The point to be conveyed is the degree of blackness possessed by her hair, rather than a degree of blackness shared by coal and her hair. For this reason we are not arrested by the introduction of coal, which simply serves a local purpose in describing or defining the blackness of her hair.

If the simile is extended into 'her hair's as black as coal dug from the darkest mine', the relationship between tenor and vehicle is altered. The extension of the vehicle intensifies the impression of blackness, but it does not do so by mere accumulation of detail, as it would if a totally different object were used as a second simile: 'her hair's as black as coal or a raven's wing'. Logically, the darkness of the mine makes no difference to the blackness of the coal dug from it. The second part of the vehicle does not intensify the suggestions of the first and thereby intensify its suggestions for the tenor. What happens is initially similar to the effect of the double comparison with coal and a raven's wing. The blackness of the coal and the darkness of the mine separately describe the colour of her hair, but because there is a prior relationship between coal and mine as product and source and because their separate qualities of blackness and darkness are combined in the woman's hair, there is a fusion of relationships and the darkness of the mine seems to be, in defiance of logic, the source of the coal's blackness. Separately, then, coal and mine are vehicles for her hair; together, her hair serves as vehicle to their tenor. As a result, the nominal tenor and vehicle are syntactically interchangeable and are therefore of equal significance.

We have, properly speaking, a creative use of language in the sense that, instead of using words simply for referential communication, the example also exploits the syntactic possibilities of word combinations both for their own sake and in order to intensify the reference value. Verse has greater opportunities for this kind of exploitation than has prose because, apart from anything else, the demands of metre and (where appropriate) of rhyme make acceptable an elliptic syntax with its contingent juxtapositions, combinations, and creative ambiguities. In predominantly assertive or descriptive writing, whether verse or prose, such creative uses of language will be local, and the overall success will be determined by how clearly and accurately the referential meaning is conveyed. In poems the language will often be predominantly creative in this sense, and the local creative uses will, commonly, be connected with each other, either creatively or discursively, to form a creative whole in which the values of the nominal vehicles will be of equal significance with the nominal tenor or tenors.

Because Dryden's poems are characteristic of the public mode, their effect derives from the way in which they reaffirm or re-create the shared assumptions of the age. Reaffirmation can be simply argued or stated, as it is in 'Religio Laici', the second part of 'The Hind and the Panther', or a prose essay like the Postscript to 'The History of the League'. Re-creation fully exploits the potential similarity of apparent dissimilars by placing the particular value to be affirmed either in the tenor or the vehicle of a comparison. The poem, that is, may talk about the nature of the constitution and illustrate it by reference to a building, or it may talk about a building and illustrate it by reference to the constitution. If it is true that a creative use of comparison effects an interchange of syntactic roles between the two halves, so that tenor illustrates vehicle in addition to vehicle illustrating tenor, then it follows that in the poetry of the public mode a creative comparison will confer the status of public value upon the superficially non-public element, whether it be found in the tenor or the vehicle: the building as well as the constitution will be of public significance. The building will not simply illustrate some aspect of the constitution, it will be interchangeable with the constitution; metaphorically it will be the constitution.

In his richly illustrated study of 'Absalom and Achitophel' Professor Schilling draws attention to the architectural metaphor in lines 801–8:

If ancient Fabricks nod, and threat to fall,
To Patch the Flaws, and Buttress up the Wall,
Thus far 'tis Duty; but here fix the Mark:
For all beyond it is to touch our Ark.
To change Foundations, cast the Frame anew,
Is work for Rebels who base Ends pursue:
At once Divine and Humane Laws controul;
And mend the Parts by ruine of the Whole.

Professor Schilling points out that 'the control of change, even when necessary, is here carried by the figure of an ancient fabric, strengthened by the religious note of sacrilege from the Old Testament ark'.[1] But Dryden's image operates more wittily and creatively than Professor Schilling indicates. Superficial amendment of the constitution is likened to minor repair of a long-established building; radical alteration of the constitution is likened to a desecration of the ark. So stated, there appear to be two distinct vehicles illustrating two aspects of a single tenor. The ark, of course, contained the God-given covenant of the Jews, their law; to lay hands on the ark accordingly represents an attempt to control divine and human laws. Indeed, the man who touched the ark died for his sacrilege, just as an attempt to overthrow the constitution is an act of high treason punishable by death. Moreover, the final resting place of the ark was within the temple. The effect of the ark reference is, then, to convert the anonymous building of the preceding couplet into the temple and consequently to realize the full spatial potential of 'beyond'. Amendment should cease with repair of the temple's outer walls; to penetrate beyond the walls to the Holy of Holies is sacrilegious rebellion and high treason. The superficially distinct vehicles are thus two aspects of the same vehicle corresponding to the two aspects of the tenor.

One convention supplies the figure of constitution as building; history supplies the conventional identity of ark and law (and hence, by extension, of the constitution); history further supplies the topographical relationship of ark and temple (itself a building). Separately, the three pairs are highly conventional; it is in their creative combination that the poetic originality resides. Once again the tenor has illustrated the vehicle as well as the vehicle the tenor, for the particular and implicit temple achieves constitutional status by attraction from the tenor in its conventional relationship with the generic and explicit building. By this means the conventional building image has been made appropriate to the episode of Jewish history which affords the poem's fable, and the relationship of part to whole is thereby emphasized.

What the ark contains is the fundamental law of the land: the constitutional relationship of king and people and the disposition of sovereignty. The walls of the temple represent the incidental manifestations of the fundamental law (the precise method of collecting taxes or electing representatives, for example). Just as the ark is within the temple, so the constitutional relationship informs the detailed workings of the law, much as the soul informs the body. In the late address to the Duchess of Ormonde, Dryden in fact used the temple and ark to convey the relationship of body and soul (lines 122–6). For this reason, the act of moving beyond the outer walls to the Holy of Holies is equivalent to

[1] Bernard N. Schilling, *Dryden and the Conservative Myth*, New Haven and London, 1961, p. 254.

a total reconstruction of the temple. The different physical reactions to the temple illustrate the same political action. Logically, the desecration of the ark and the reconstruction of the temple are not equivalent, but by uniting them in the nominal tenor they are given a metaphoric truth similar to that of black coal and dark mines.

Dryden in this passage uses metaphor as analogy: the equivalence of tenor and vehicle is confirmed by arguing that point for point correspondence between two objects or qualities which is the special property of analogy. Professor Wimsatt has suggested that analogy is found in a comparison between objects of the same species, metaphor in a comparison between objects of different species:[2] Charles II is analogous to King David and metaphorically a lion. It is true that the equivalence of the two halves and the logical working out of correspondence will most readily obtain in the circumstances described by Professor Wimsatt. But Dryden's characteristic poetic is most successful when his comparisons achieve the status of analogy as I have described it. Whatever their superficial differences, in Dryden's works the same poetic effect is achieved by likening Charles to David or a lion and by likening the English constitution to the Roman or a building. The function of the biblical fable in 'Absalom and Achitophel' is similar to the function of the beast fable in 'The Hind and the Panther': both the kingdom of Jews and the kingdom of beasts will serve to illustrate the kingdom of England.

One way of defining specifically creative analogy is to find it in comparisons where an established or agreed likeness between two objects is shown to be of greater extent and significance than was initially realized. The prior agreement will then derive from the fact that the objects are of the same species or from the fact that objects of different species are already linked in the common figurative awareness of the age, as were constitutions with buildings and as are nuclear explosions with mushrooms. The long inventory of commonplace analogies drawn up by Professor Schilling thus has value in making available to twentieth-century readers the source material of much of Dryden's poetry. It simplifies the task of appreciating the poetry by permitting a concentration upon the way in which the commonplaces are extended and re-created rather than merely reflected.

To achieve a working out of correspondence that maintains the equivalent public significance of the two halves of a comparison, Dryden often modifies the referential terms of the tenor or the vehicle (as is the case with the Jacob allusion in the lines to his cousin). When this equivalence is not maintained, when the vehicle merely illustrates a proposition or description instead of conveying and enlarging upon it, Dryden's poetry is usually unsuccessful. It is in these terms that the

[2] W. K. Wimsatt, Jr, *The Verbal Icon*, Lexington, Kentucky, 1954, pp. 149–50.

general failure (if partial success) of 'Annus Mirabilis' should be considered.

All critics of Dryden have drawn attention to his skill in verse argument. Like many good arguers, Dryden operates most effectively when working from and exploring the implications of an agreed basic premise, whether logical or figurative. He is less successful in establishing a new basic premise and then arguing from that. He is less successful, in fact, when handling images which lack the force of established analogy.

Both Dryden and Donne were skilled in verse argument; both drew much of their material from conventional, if different sources. At his best Donne modifies his material into a new first premise from which to work out his argument. At his best Dryden restates an existing first premise from which to work out the analogous correspondences. In seventeenth-century terms, Dryden's invention, his finding of ideas and images, is usually less exciting than Donne's because it is, in twentieth-century terms, less inventive. Donne is a master of the private, Dryden of the public mode. With Donne we are aware of a new individual experience suggesting general relevance; with Dryden we respond to an original reworking or re-creation of matters of established general relevance. When, in some of his early poems, Dryden attempts a Donnean new first premise, the result is often unconvincing because he fails to establish as equivalent the two halves of his comparison. Because he apparently lacked the individual perception of similarity between dissimilars, Dryden's so-called metaphysical mode in the early work usually produces a subordination of vehicle to tenor in which a reader is chiefly conscious of an unsuccessful and over-ingenious attempt to unite the disparate. Donne's individual perception has general relevance to other individuals as individuals; Dryden's public perception has general relevance to other individuals as members of the public.

This distinction may be briefly illustrated. When in 'The Sun Rising' Donne celebrates the relationship between himself and his mistress by proclaiming that 'She'is all States, and all Princes, I,/Nothing else is', his assertion has, despite the source of the metaphor, no political reverberations. The neoplatonic idealism of 'The Sun Rising' permits the poet to subsume all external values into the wholly private relationship with his mistress. In this ironic aubade the man and woman have responsibilities only to each other, and none to the inhabitants of the expanding landscape outside the window: the city prentices, the court huntsmen riding on the outskirts of the metropolis, the labourers deep in the country, the East and West Indies. The view from this room, which the lovers do not in any case take, expands only to contract again. The poem's situation, the coherent attitude it expresses, has significance for the individual solely as individual. But when David begets Absalom with 'diviner Lust' and 'a greater Gust', the private pleasure he experiences is overshadowed by the public consequences of his careless promiscuity: the threat to the royal succession from the bastard prince. Similarly, Achitophel's demonstration of virility results in a son 'Got, while his Soul did hudled Notions try;/And born a shapeless Lump, like Anarchy'. Achitophel's fatherhood is but one more evidence of his dangerous public character: the anarchically shapeless body of his son is symbolic of the consequence of Achitophel's plots against the body politic of Israel. Even in their more intimate moments, then, the characters in Dryden's poem are seen in terms of their public status, and the poem's attitudes accordingly have significance for individuals as members of the public. . . .

The possibility is a further reminder that in the public mode of Dryden a creative and witty use of analogy often consists in effecting a correspondence between analogies drawn from different sources and applied to the same object or tenor. Thus, 'The Medal' not only illustrates affairs in England by reference to affairs in heaven, it also draws upon the rich stock of natural analogies in the shape of beast and monster images or allusions to the climate theory of government, while at one point the poem makes use of aesthetic analogy when rebellious disorder in the state is conveyed by the disorderly freedom of verse: 'Nor Faith nor Reason make thee at a stay,/Thou leapst o'r all eternal truths, in thy *Pindarique* way!' Characteristically, the second line both asserts the Pindaric's destruction of neoclassical restraint and illustrates it by allowing the line to spill over into a fourteener. Aesthetic analogy, of course, draws upon music, painting, poetry and architecture, each with its appropriate forms and abuses to correspond with law and disorder in the state.

I have no wish to duplicate the work of Professor Schilling in a general account of the various neoclassical analogies: human, divine, natural and aesthetic, with such subspecies as medical, scientific, astrological, geographic, or mythological. I believe, in any case, that the analogies are most properly discussed in their individual poetic contexts, for it is only there that we can determine whether the commonplaces are merely reflected or wittily re-created and extended. An exception may be made, however, in the case of the important group of analogies drawn from history.

The place and significance of historical allusion in seventeenth-century poetry is a subject of sufficient magnitude to justify a separate study, and in noting some points of relevance to Dryden's work my account will inevitably simplify the general context. Concern with a poet's relative originality suggests that the first point to be emphasized is the greater freedom of invention permitted him by the nature of historical allusion than by other available analogies. In history we have to deal with analogy as defined by Professor Wimsatt; and because the agreed initial likeness here consists in comparison between objects of the same species, variations upon historical analogy are as wide as a poet's reading and the demands of his poem will allow. History will furnish whole galleries of representative tyrants and just rulers, while nature supplies comparatively few political types from the kingdom of beasts, and these types derive most of their force from an existing conventional usage of just those examples.

It is true that certain characters and episodes from history were more frequently applied than others to similar situations in the seventeenth century. Largely because of the success of Dryden's poem, the popularity of Achitophel's intrigue is perhaps the best known example. But there were many historical precedents of equivalent popularity, and a random selection might include David's exile, Caesar's defeat of Pompey, the Catholic League of sixteenth-century France, and the succession of Edward III. The existing popularity of such allusions as illustrations of the same contemporary event frequently adds local or general complexity to Dryden's poems by calling upon the established topical application, although it must be reiterated that such pre-existent values should be applied with caution to specific poems. One reason for the possible reference of 'Alexander's Feast' to William III's defeat of James II is that opponents and supporters of the revolutionary settlement occasionally sought historical authority for their arguments in, among other places, the conscientious obligations of Darius's Jewish subjects when he had been defeated by Alexander. The prior association of William and James with Alexander and Darius thus increases the topical potential of Dryden's ode, a potential which it does not realize.

Such a selection of popular precedents as that offered in the previous paragraph is an indication that history indifferently concerned itself with events from the Creation through the four empires of Assyria, Persia, Greece, and Rome. Historical allusion covered references to Noah's ark, Scipio's defeat of Hannibal, and the events of the Great Rebellion. Ralegh's *History of the World* was ambitious less for its intended scope than for the detail in which he proposed to treat each empire. A similar project was entertained by William Howell, historiographer-royal during the Restoration, in his *Institution of General History*, while one of the most popular works of the period was John Sleidan's handbook on the four empires. In such a context the most frequently cited portions of the Bible were Genesis, in which the first institution of government could be observed, and the historical books of the Old Testament with the supplementary material of Josephus, for in them were observable the constitutional implications of the practical working of government.

The quantity of historical allusion in his poems would itself testify to Dryden's interest, and in his 'Character of Polybius' he endorsed the high status of history in humanistic studies during the Renaissance and seventeenth century.[3] Dryden succeeded Howell as historiographer-royal in 1670, and although the duties of this office during the Restora-

---

[3] George Watson, ed., *Essays*, 1962, Vol. 2, p. 68. Unless otherwise stated the place of publication is London.

tion were as ambiguous as those of the laureateship to which he was appointed in 1668, it seems clear that it involved among other things the use of historical knowledge for royal propaganda.[4] Dryden's most considerable production as historiographer was the translation of Maimbourg's *History of the League* (1684), the chief point of which is apparently contained in the long Postscript drawing out the implications of the League for the recent Exclusion crisis and the Whig proposal for a Protestant Association to keep the royal succession from the Roman Catholic James Duke of York. Two years earlier Dryden had collaborated with Lee on *The Duke of Guise*, a dramatic version of the League with similar topical implications.

The view of history supporting these multiple allusions is the theory that history affords abundant examples of God's providential plan for the world. As Ralegh expressed it: 'the judgements of GOD are for ever unchangeable; neither is he wearied by the long processe of time, and won to give his blessing in one age, to that which he hath cursed in another. Wherefore those that are wise . . . will bee able to discerne the bitter fruites of irreligious policie, as well among those examples that are found in ages removed farre from the present, as in those of latter times.' More succinctly, 'the examples of divine providence, every where found . . . have perswaded me to fetch my beginning from the beginning of all things; to wit, Creation'.[5]

Because history chiefly meant a record of such public events as the rise and fall of princes and governments, battles, treaties, and rebellions, the precedents it afforded were more often political than ethical. There is consequently a frequent and striking resemblance between treatises of government and works of history. Ralegh is for ever interrupting his chronicle to point the precept implied by some past event, while many tracts of political theory conduct their case by hopping from one historical precedent to another. The most influential work of Jean Bodin was the *République*, a vast compendium of royalist theory, but he had earlier written a Latin treatise with the engaging title of a *Method for the Easy Comprehension of History*. Predictably, the *Methodus* deduces the grounds of government from an historical survey, while the *République* is, apart from its sheer bulk, chiefly remarkable for the facility with which it supplies precedents for even the most trivial of constitutional principles.

There were, in fact, three main versions of the inevitable connection between history and governmental theory: the chronicle with digressive pointing of political precept; the political treatise with historical illustrations; the chronicle with a topical application in preface or postscript. In the first, governmental theory is a major justification for the writing of history; in the second, historical precedent affords authority for

[4] Roswell G. Ham, 'Dryden as Historiographer-Royal', *RES*, 11, 1935, pp. 284–98.

[5] Ralegh, *The History of the World*, 1614, A3r, D2r: italics reversed.

governmental theory; in the third, history and theory are mutually dependent for their value. Political poetry most often adapted the second version, although *The Duke of Guise* is more appropriate to the third and 'Absalom and Achitophel' (like Dryden's projected epic on the subject of Arthur or the Black Prince[6]) is most properly seen as an adaptation of the first with elements of the third.

A characteristic example of this connection is a tract of 1661 entitled *Semper Iidem: or, a Parallel betwixt the Ancient and Modern Fanatics*, in which the age's favourite historical game is played with the aid of a conventional double column matching old and new fanatics. History is used as a species of proof: you take from the past a known fanatic, tyrant, or traitor, and, by pointing out the resemblances between his actions and those of a contemporary, 'prove' the contemporary's fanaticism, tyranny, or treason. The cogency of the argument consists in the detail with which the parallel is worked out; and *parallel* in this context is virtually synonymous with *analogy* as I have described it.

'Our Play's a Parallel', is the confident opening of the Prologue to *The Duke of Guise*:

> The Holy League
> Begot our Cov'nant: Guisards got the Whigg:
> Whate'er our hot-brain'd Sheriffs did advance,
> Was, like our Fashions, first produc'd in *France*.

Just as an observed similarity in their grounds for insurrection inspired royalists to remark an apparently indissoluble union between old (Jesuit) priest and new (republican) presbyter, so the 1680's witnessed a similarly untiring insistence on the connection between old Guisard and new Whig, between old Catholic League and new Protestant Association. In the year that saw the production of *The Duke of Guise*, John Northleigh made use of the equally popular analogy between the Association and the Solemn League and Covenant of Civil War days in his conventionally named treatise, *The Parallel, or the New Specious Association an Old Rebellious Covenant*. When, in 1685, Northleigh followed up this work with *The Triumph of our Monarchy over the Plots and Principles of our Rebels and Republicans*, Dryden began his commendatory verses on the two pieces with the following lines:

> So *Joseph* yet a youth, expounded well ⎫
> The bodeing Dream, and did th'event foretell, ⎬
> Judg'd by the past, and drew the Parallel. ⎭
> Thus early *Solomon* the Truth explor'd,
> The Right awarded, and the Babe restor'd.

Characteristically, the implicit parallel Dryden himself fashions between the judgement of Solomon and the restoration of Charles II is only

---

[6] *Essays*, ed., Watson, Vol. 2, pp. 91–2.

possible in the elliptic brevity of verse. Simply by using the charged word 'restored' the lines permit a witty reference which is, as Sidney would say, not explicitly affirmed and therefore no lie. A conscientious historian in prose would be hard put to argue the validity of Dryden's implication, and with such resources at his disposal a poet obviously possesses greater opportunities for the witty invention (in both the old and the current senses) of historical parallels and analogies.

Equally of note is the proposition contained in the opening triplet. If, as Ralegh believed, like actions in different ages are judged alike by God, then an accurate identification of a present with a past act provides the basis for predicting the outcome of the present along the lines of the observed outcome of the past. Thus, Ralegh borrowed the Augustinian division of providence into memory of the past, knowledge of the present, and care for the future. Thus, too, Dryden's brother-in-law, Sir Robert Howard, remarked in the 1690 preface to his history of Edward II and Richard II that, having 'perceiv'd how exactly they [Charles II and James II] follow'd the steps of these two unfortunate Kings . . . I then expected to see a Revolution resembling theirs'.[7] This application of history is similar to the rhetorical figure of paradigm, Puttenham's 'resemblance by example', through which 'we compare the past with the present, gathering probabilitie of like successe to come in things wee have presently in hand'. Interestingly, Puttenham found paradigm to consist also in 'examples of bruite beastes, aptly corresponding in qualitie or event' to some man or human activity.[8] As I mentioned, there is a similar rhetorical equivalence between Dryden's comparing Charles with a lion and with David.

Dryden's poems abound with prophecies, usually explicit, and they have no air of the visionary because they are customarily supported by a prudent consideration of the lessons of history. 'Astraea Redux' ends, as its title warns, with a *pax Romana* vision of England's future greatness based upon Charles II's analogous relationship with Augustus. The contemporaneous address to Sir Robert Howard predicts the success of his volume of poems because the star of Charles II's restored fortune is fixed in its horoscope. The astrological image is converted into astronomy at the end of the panegyric on Clarendon eighteen months later with the Chancellor in orbit about a solar Charles, thus permitting the poet to prophesy, rather incautiously as it turned out, that Clarendon's career would be as enduringly successful as his royal master's. 'Annus Mirabilis' borrows the apocalyptic golden age of Revelation to predict the future prosperity of a London purged by the fire of 1666. 'Absalom and Achitophel' repeats the closing vision of 'Astraea Redux', while the peroration of 'The Medal' commences with an assurance that 'Without a

---

[7] *The History of the Reigns of Edward and Richard II*, 1690, p. iii.

[8] Puttenham, *Arte of English Poesie*, ed. G. D. Willcock and A. Walker, Cambridge, 1936, Vol. 3, Chapter 19, pp. 245–6.

Vision Poets can fore-show/What all but Fools, by common Sense may know'. The fables of the swallows and the pigeons in the third part of 'The Hind and the Panther' represent rival predictions of the outcome of James II's religious policy and the popular reaction to it.

The useful relevance of prophecy to the poetic praise of great men had been demonstrated for all time by Virgil's fourth Eclogue and the Messianic books of the Old Testament, but for the public poet of the Restoration, with his rational distrust of inspiration, the lessons of history permitted a significant modification of the tradition of the poet as vates and allowed him to predict without incurring the odium of a visionary.

Since most of Dryden's original poems were exercises in praise (or its rhetorical converse of vituperation), historical analogy functions in them most obviously as a source of rhetorical amplification, by which a man is compared with others of known worth (or infamy) and proved equal or superior to them. His poems sometimes appear to comprise little more than a series of eulogistic or denigrative parallels, meriting a loud Johnsonian snort about servile flattery. At his best, however, Dryden effects internal relevance between many of the analogies he employs, and the consistently argued historical parallel gives his work both general and local complexity. Most strikingly, 'Absalom and Achitophel' turns the process inside out and ensures the consistency of the vehicle by making it, in effect, the practical tenor. In general, amplification of the king's exploits is achieved by analogy with the exploits of past kings, whereas amplification of the exploits of the less great (poets, politicians, or scholars) draws indifferently upon the example of past and present rulers.

Again and again, Dryden's complimentary addresses to his friends and fellow poets are couched in terms that shape the recipient's achievement into the image of England's current constitutional activity and situation. Sir Robert Howard's restoration of poetry to its rightful dominion over 'Morall Knowledge' is analogous to the restoration of Charles to his rightful dominion over England. The witty exploitation of an analogy between affairs in the kingdom of letters and the kingdom of England does not simply afford the poem complexity and integrity. The establishment of equivalence between the two halves of the comparison both magnifies (or amplifies) the public significance of poetry and demonstrates the interconnection of all activities in the land. The stability of the monarchy assures the security of the individual, the flourishing of the arts, and the prosperity of the nation (conversely, the flourishing of the arts argues the stability of the monarchy). No matter how well such artifacts as buildings and engines may serve to illustrate the constitution, the analogy which finally underlies all other analogies is the commonplace association of the human and political bodies. Philosophically the age expressed itself in mechanistic terms, and these terms supplied it with many an incidental image, but its view of the matter which most exercised its poets, the place and obligations of man

E

in the state, was characteristically and conventionally conveyed in terms of an organic analogy.

From 'Analogies for Poetry', in *Dryden's Poetic Kingdoms*, London, 1965, pp. 15–34 (15–21, 27–34).

All for Love

In his Preface to *All for Love* Dryden claims that he wrote his play for 'the excellency of the moral: For the chief persons represented, were famous patterns of unlawful love; and their end accordingly was unfortunate'. However, the play does not picture criminal love punished for voluntary transgression. It pictures a transcendent love for which, as the play's subtitle states, the world is well lost. We do not judge the hero and the heroine; rather at the play's conclusion they receive our pity, and because of this their passion seems inevitable, correct, and vindicated. Clearly there is a difference between Dryden's announced purpose and what he wrote. This difference can be explained and a clearer picture of his intentions emerges, if we realize that Dryden's idea of drama was going through a transition at this time, and that the Preface to *All for Love* reflects more than one influence. In the Epistle Dedicatory to *Aureng-Zebe* Dryden states his dissatisfaction with the contemporary stage: 'I am weary with drawing the deformities of life, and lazars of the people, where every figure of imperfection more resembles me than it can do others. If I must be condemned to rhyme, I should find some ease in my change of punishment. I desire to be no longer the Sisyphus of the stage; to roll up a stone with endless labour, (which, to follow the proverb, gathers no moss) and which is perpetually falling down again.' Dryden wished to move away from the heroic play, with its baggage of epic theory, French moral idealism, and Caroline wit; but the major problem that he faced was that the rigid neoclassical theories of Thomas Rymer were favoured by Rochester and the Court wits. In the Preface to *All for Love* Dryden attacks his opponents for judging his play by French rules of decorum: 'Their [French] heroes are the most civil people breathing; but their good breeding seldom extends to a word of sense; all their wit is in their ceremony; they want the genius which animates our stage; and there-fore it is but necessary, when they cannot please, that they should take care not to offend.' About the perfect, or ideal, hero of French drama Dryden says: 'their Hippolitus is so scrupulous in point of decency, that he will rather expose himself to death, than accuse his step-mother to his father; and my critics I am sure will commend him for it: But we of grosser apprehensions are apt to think, that this excess of generosity is not practicable, but with fools and madmen.' Behind Dryden's attack on decorum there are some important critical assumptions, the most important of which is his belief that the emotions raised in the audience towards the protagonist are of more importance than the formal structure of drama. Dryden believes that a major end of tragedy is to create pity for the hero. The Aristotelian language should not mislead us: 'All reasonable men have long since concluded, that the hero of the poem ought not to be a character of perfect virtue, for then he could not, without injustice, be made unhappy; nor yet altogether wicked, because he could not then be pitied.'

The disagreement between the professional dramatists led by Dryden and the courtiers led by Rochester is a reflection of the changes which took place within French neoclassical theory during the early 1670s, when the rigid formalism predominant in the Academy was modified by Rapin, Boileau, and Le Bossu. Some notes Dryden made during this time, 'Heads of an Answer to Rymer's Remarks on the Tragedies of the Last Age' (1677), show that he fully accepted the new, liberal views of Rapin. Against Rymer's claim that there is no source of tragedy but pity and terror, Dryden cites Rapin's defence of love as a subject for drama. Where Rymer says that the plot is the soul of tragedy, Dryden counters this with Rapin's authority for the importance of 'words and discourse': 'Rapin's words are remarkable:—It is not the admirable intrigue, the surprising events, and the extraordinary incidents, that make the beauty of a tragedy; it is the discourses, when they are natural and passionate.' After Dryden rejected the heroic style, 'natural and passionate' discourses became central to his purpose. This approach towards drama also offered a critical justification for his interest in Shakespeare: 'for the raising of Shakespeare's passions are more from the excellency of the words and thoughts than the justness of the occasion; and if he has been able to pick single occasions, he has never founded the whole reasonably; yet by the genius of poetry in writing, he has succeeded'.

Dryden's later dramatic criticism is based on Rapin's claim that the function of the pity and terror raised by tragedy is to create compassion: 'The pity which the poet is to labour for is for the criminal, not for those or him whom he has murdered, or who have been the occasion of the tragedy. The terror is likewise in the punishment of the same criminal, who, if he be represented too great an offender, will not be pitied; if altogether innocent, his punishment will be unjust'. A more complete exposition of Dryden's views is in 'The Grounds of Criticism in Tragedy' (1679):

> Rapin, a judicious critic, has observed from Aristotle that pride and want of commiseration are the most predominant vices in mankind; therefore, to cure us of these two, the inventors of tragedy have chosen to work upon two other passions, which are, fear and pity. We are wrought to fear, by their setting before our eyes some terrible example of misfortune, which happened to persons of the highest quality; for such an action demonstrates to us, that no condition is privileged from the turns of fortune; this must of necessity cause terror in us, and

consequently abate our pride. But when we see that the most virtuous, as well as the greatest, are not exempt from such misfortunes, that consideration moves pity in us, and insensibly works us to be helpful to, and tender over, the distressed; which is the noblest and most godlike of moral virtues.

And yet if *All for Love* owes its power to techniques which gain our sympathy for Antony and Cleopatra, it is in some ways less satisfactory than Dryden's other plays for that very reason. Emotion is a powerful weapon which, while vitally necessary to literature, must go hand in hand with intelligence. Without intelligence art tends towards the soft and vague: plots become arbitrary, and characters not sufficiently motivated in their actions and passions. By intelligence, I do not mean the holding of ideas and the ability intellectually to defend them. I mean the whole personality of the author, with his feelings, opinions, beliefs, and insights into man, society, and the divine.

Normally the values conveyed by Dryden's works tend to be more limiting than expressive, and therefore most suitable to such forms as satire and the moral fable. Such plays as *The Conquest of Granada* and *Marriage à la Mode* might be considered satires of expressive values. Even when ideas are directly stated as in *The State of Innocence*, the values are still those of limitation and self-regulation. Such values are lacking in *All for Love*. Instead we feel the emotional suggestiveness of many fine lines and scenes; but taken as a whole the play lacks any further dimensions of vision. Upon successive readings *All for Love* diminishes in interest.

Eventually we begin to ask what the point of *All for Love* is. Once we have grasped how easily Antony's love wins over his duty there is no real conflict left to engage our intelligence. Caesar's role has been reduced to a reminder of the least attractive of Roman values:

O, 'tis the coldest youth upon a Charge,
The most deliberate fighter! if he ventures
(As in *Illyria* once they say he did
To storm a Town) 'tis when he cannot chuse,
When all the World have fixt their eyes upon him;
And then he lives on that for seven years after,
But, at a close revenge he never fails.[1]

Octavia could have offered a true conflict between passion and duty to Antony; but Dryden's fear that she would lessen the favour of the audience towards Antony and Cleopatra resulted in making her a prude to whom pleasure is a sin:

Far be their knowledge from a *Roman* Lady,
Far from a modest Wife. Shame of our Sex,

[1] *All for Love*, II, i, 19.

> Dost thou not blush, to own those black endearments
> That make sin pleasing?[2]

What then remains to drive Antony from Cleopatra but his honour, an honour without purpose? And what issue is really at stake? Certainly not Antony's love nor Cleopatra's honesty, but whether Antony will leave Cleopatra to fight for a world not worth having.

Despite the fine emotional language many scenes are not sufficiently motivated. After Ventidius has persuaded Antony to go to war again, Cleopatra attempts to regain him. Her speeches are excellent:

> How shall I plead my cause, when you, my Judge
> Already have condemn'd me? Shall I bring
> The Love you bore me for my Advocate?
> That now is turn'd against me, that destroys me;
> For, love once past, is, at the best, forgotten;
> But oftner sours to hate: 'twill please my Lord
> To ruine me, and therefore I'll be guilty.[3]

But what do they speak about? Not the necessities of the time, not weakening love, not self-preservation, nor kingdom, nor honour; rather that Cleopatra was once Julius Caesar's mistress:

> You seem griev'd,
> (And therein you are kind) that *Caesar* first
> Enjoy'd my love, though you deserv'd it better:
> I grieve for that, my Lord, much more than you;
> For, had I first been yours, it would have sav'd
> My second choice: I never had been his,
> And ne'r had been but yours. But *Caesar* first,
> You say, possess'd my love. Not so, my Lord:
> He first possess'd my Person; you my Love:
> *Caesar* lov'd me; but I lov'd *Antony*.
> If I endur'd him after, 'twas because
> I judg'd it due to the first name of Men;
> And, half constrain'd, I gave, as to a Tyrant,
> What he would take by force.[4]

It is only necessary for her to show Antony an offer from Caesar that she has refused, and his reason is overcome again by love. Why, we may ask, does Antony require Dollabella to give Cleopatra his farewell, except that Dryden felt it was a pathetic touch? Certainly these speeches were meant to draw sentiment from the audience, and lack Dryden's customary intelligence to restrain the emotion:

> DOLLABELLA   Then let *Ventidius*;
>   He's rough by nature.

[2] *All for Love*, III, i, 43.
[3] *All for Love*, II, i, 25.
[4] *All for Love*, II, i, 26.

ANTONY Oh, he'll speak too harshly;
  He'll kill her with the news: Thou, only thou.
DOLLABELLA Nature has cast me in so soft a mould,
  That but to hear a story feign'd for pleasure
  Of some sad Lovers death, moistens my eyes,
  And robs me of my Manhood.—I should speak
  So faintly; with such fear to grieve her heart,
  She'd not believe it earnest.[5]

Stuff for parody, the sentiments of which would be speedily demolished in the heroic plays by ironic imagery; but here Dryden means it seriously. And even the suicide scene, which is the obvious crown of the play, is a series of awkward sentimentalities leading to:

See, see how the Lovers sit in State together,
As they were giving Laws to half Mankind.
Th' impression of a smile left in her face,
Shows she dy'd pleas'd with him for whom she liv'd,
And went to charm him in another World.[6]

All for Love succeeds as Dryden wished: in the predominance of passion over reason, the heightened language which raises our emotions, and, most important, the achievement of sympathy and compassion for the errors of the main characters. If we see the raising of emotional sympathy for Antony and Cleopatra as Dryden's intention, then many other seeming confusions in *All for Love* disappear. The suicide of Ventidius, the cold virtue of Octavia, and the lack of moral judgement in the play's conclusion add to the sympathy Dryden hoped to achieve for his hero and heroine. Within its limited purpose, the play is nearly perfect and justifies our study. Dryden's aims, however, were insufficient; *All for Love* misses greatness because its main concern is rather with raising the spectator's emotions than with the inspection of life. If Rapin's theories were useful for constructing a play, they also had the unfortunate side effect of filtering Dryden's personality out of his writing. *All for Love* consequently lacks any pressure of intelligence operating upon its subject-matter, and we are left with a feeling of having been cheated. *All for Love*, however, taught Dryden how to create passionate scenes and raise emotions, and it settled his dramatic language. Each of Dryden's major plays in the future will bear the marks of his experiments here.

A question remains. Why did Dryden say that he wrote *All for Love* for the excellency of its moral? This was a period of transition when his critical principles were unsettled and when he was concerned with finding less constricting rules. After Dryden broke with the formula of the heroic play he not only was influenced by those elements in Rapin's epic theory which seemed a justification for the romantic side of drama,

---

[5] *All for Love*, IV, i, 45.
[6] *All for Love*, V, i, 78.

but a little later he came under the moralizing influence of Le Bossu. In 'The Grounds of Criticism in Tragedy' Dryden cites Rapin's observation that the purpose of tragedy is to move the viewer's pity for the misfortunes of the distressed: 'When the soul becomes agitated with fear for one character, or hope for another; then it is that we are pleased in tragedy.' This could apply to *All for Love*. However, Dryden also cites the authority of Le Bossu ('the best of modern critics'): 'The first rule which Bossu prescribes to the writer of an heroic poem, and which holds too by the same reason in all dramatic poetry, is to make the moral of the work; that is, to lay down to yourself what that precept of morality shall be, which you would insinuate into the people; as namely, Homer's (which I have copied in my "Conquest of Granada") was, that union preserves a commonwealth, and discord destroys it. Sophocles in his Oedipus, that no man is to be accounted happy before his death.'

It is probable that in his Preface to *All for Love* Dryden had in mind Le Bossu's concept of drama as a moral fable. But, if so, why did he apply it to a play which was based upon a different critical theory? I think the above passages clear up the problem. *The Conquest of Granda* no more insinuates 'that union preserves a commonwealth, and discord destroys it' than *All for Love* demonstrates the unfortunate end of unlawful love. It seems likely that Dryden had no sooner discovered Le Bossu's theories than he tried to reinterpret his plays by them. I think that the Preface to *All for Love* is the first example of Le Bossu's influence on Dryden and that Dryden either did not completely understand Le Bossu's ideas or he superficially appropriated them as counters in his disagreement with the courtiers. The real influence of Le Bossu will be seen later in *The Spanish Friar* (1680) and *Don Sebastian* (1689).

From Chapter 8 of *Dryden's Major Plays*, Edinburgh and London, 1966, pp. 133–47 (140–7).

The Sceptical Critic

Most discussions of Dryden's characteristic thought are governed by a set of assumptions about his scepticism and its relation to his other ideas which have been accepted, with very few exceptions, by most students of the poet for the past thirty years. This conception of Dryden is so familiar that it can be reviewed very briefly.

It begins with the hypothesis that Dryden was a Pyrrhonist, or anti-rationalist, and proceeds to use this hypothesis to explain his public behaviour and poetic thought in a great many widely different areas. Dryden – so runs the explanation – was not so much unable to make up his mind as unwilling to do so. The most significant parallel to this attitude is to be found in the essays of Montaigne, and its intellectual antecedents are to be sought in the two-thousand-year-old tradition of philosophical scepticism. Since Dryden was convinced that reason and the senses are essentially unreliable, he concluded that knowledge is uncertain and speculation vain. Unwilling to commit himself on any questions to which more than one answer could be suggested, he had recourse to that perennial suspension of judgement which Montaigne recommends in his essays by precept and example.

Once we view Dryden in this light (it is suggested) much that was previously obscure in his writings or inexplicable in his behaviour will become clear and consistent. Thus, his habit of juxtaposing positions which are contrary to each other, as in 'An Essay of Dramatic Poesy' and 'The Hind and the Panther', will be seen to be the confirmed sceptics' penchant for balancing conflicting opinions. Again, Dryden's political conservatism can be explained as a fear of change and a distrust of novelty to which he was predisposed by his philosophical scepticism. For it is a corollary of the distrust of human reason that the Pyrrhonist casts a sceptical eye upon Utopias, ideas of reform, and suggestions for human betterment. Such plans are, in his view, as chimerical as any other speculations, and not worth exchanging for the established system of government at the cost of upheavals and possibly even bloodshed. Thus we should expect the sceptic to be just such a supporter of stable forms of government as Dryden in fact is. Finally, Dryden's conversion to the Catholic faith will cease to draw accusations of inconsistency and time-serving once we perceive that this was merely the highly predictable outcome of a long search for infallible authority as a substitute for fallible reason in matters of religion.[1]

It has been some years since this interpretation was first offered, and its wide acceptance in recent years is undeniable. In biographies of Dryden, in editions of his poems, and in studies of his individual works, his Pyrrhonism has become one of those commonplaces, like the date of his birth or the shortcomings of his wife, to which reference can be made, but for which no further proof need be attempted.[2] We can easily guess at some, at least, of the reasons for the popularity of this hypothesis. It offers, as no other theory has been able to do, a single, relatively simple explanation for a highly complex series of thoughts and actions for which Dryden was responsible. It allows us to predict these in advance, as logical consequences of Dryden's anti-rationalism, much as we can produce corollaries from a given proposition. 'It is obvious', we are told, 'that the man who in that century found himself inclined to philosophical scepticism was likely to find his views to some extent determined thereby in such distantly related subjects as religion and politics'.[3] Clearly, Dryden's Pyrrhonism is a premise which leads to many conclusions.

Sceptics—of a rather different kind—have nevertheless been heard to complain, from time to time, that some of these conclusions seem to be derived from altogether different premises. It has been some years since Hoyt Trowbridge argued that the theoretical foundations of Dryden's criticism suggested a mind which had been schooled not in philosophical scepticism but upon the logical treatises of Aristotle.[4] More recently, two critics, working independently, have both suggested

[1] The fullest argument for this view is presented by Louis I. Bredvold, *The Intellectual Milieu of John Dryden*, University of Michigan Press, Ann Arbor, 1934.

[2] See, for example, *The Best of Dryden*, ed. Louis I. Bredvold, Thomas Nelson, New York, 1933, pp. xxvi–xxxiv; Mildred E. Hartsock, 'Dryden's Plays: A Study in Ideas', *Seventeenth Century Studies, Second Series*, ed. Robert Shafer, Princeton University Press, Princeton, 1937, pp. 71–176; James M. Osborn, *John Dryden: Some Biographical Facts and Problems*, Columbia University Press, New York, 1940, p. 106; *The Poetical Works of Dryden*, ed. George R. Noyes, 2nd ed., Houghton Mifflin Co., Boston, 1950, pp. xlix–l; Bonamy Dobrée, *John Dryden*, Longmans, London, 1956, pp. 10–12; Charles E. Ward, *The Life of John Dryden*, University of North Carolina Press, Chapel Hill, 1961, p. 15; *Selected Poems of John Dryden*, ed. Roger Sharrock, William Heinemann, London, 1963, p. 6; Selma Assir Zebouni, *Dryden: A Study in Heroic Characterization*, Louisiana State University Press, Baton Rouge, 1965, pp. 43–5. Miss Hartsock's study is intended as an 'extension' to Professor Bredvold's, and she devotes an entire chapter to Montaigne's influence on Dryden; yet she consistently identifies the latter's 'Pyrrhonism' with religious scepticism, or agnosticism (see, for example, pp. 160 and 173–6). Her views are therefore much closer to those of Sir Walter Scott (see *The Works of John Dryden*, ed. Sir Walter Scott and George Saintsbury, William Paterson, Edinburgh, 1882–93, Vol. 1, p. 263 [hereafter referred to as *Works*]).

[3] Bredvold, *Intellectual Milieu*, p. 153.

[4] See his very perceptive study of 'The Place of Rules in Dryden's Criticism', *Modern Philology*, 44, 1946, pp. 84–96.

that Dryden's views in 'Religio Laici' owe nothing to the tradition of Christian scepticism.[5]

Doubts such as these concern the consistency between some of Dryden's articulated ideas and the anti-rationalism which is supposed to be responsible for them. Similar difficulties occur when we consider whether Dryden's public behaviour is consistent with his supposed allegiance to Pyrrhonism. For one thing, the conservatism for which the sceptic is notorious in politics has its counterpart in religion. Montaigne, so often cited as a kind of paradigm of Christian scepticism, could boast that as a consequence of his Pyrrhonism he enjoyed 'a certain steadfastness of opinion' and had 'not much altered those that were original and native with me'. This had produced the same tranquillity in religion as he pursued in politics. 'In this way I have, by the grace of God, with no perturbation and disturbance of conscience, preserved my faith intact in the ancient beliefs of our religion, amid so many sects and divisions that our age has produced.'[6] That faith was the Catholic one, since he lived in France. But who can doubt that if Montaigne had lived in England and belonged to the Established Church, the same attitude would have made him hold fast to the state religion of that country and reject all those sects, including the Catholic one, which threatened its tranquillity? Dryden's behaviour, in leaving the Established Church to join and stubbornly adhere to a despised and persecuted minority, is so contrary to this as to be inexplicable if he was indeed of Montaigne's mind.

Or again, the hypothesis that Dryden was a Pyrrhonist does not accord at all well with the frequent and enthusiastic praise he offers the new science and the contempt he expresses for that of the ancients. Montaigne, confronted with the arguments between the Copernicans and the supporters of the Ptolemaic system, could only wonder: 'What lesson does this have for us, except that it does not matter to us which of the two opinions is true? And who knows but that a third, a thousand years hence, will overthrow the two former?'[7] In contrast to such studied indifference, Dryden can only exclaim that freeborn reason, long enslaved by the ancients, has at last been set at liberty by the new philosophy to accomplish the hopeful predictions he makes for it.

These may not be decisive objections to the theory of Dryden's Pyrrhonism, although I suspect that any attempt to answer them effectively would require appeals to that very quality of inconsistency in Dryden's character which this theory was designed to disprove. What these objections do suggest, however, is that this hypothesis does not 'solve the phenomena', as Dryden's contemporaries would have

[5] See Elias J. Chiasson, 'Dryden's Apparent Scepticism in "Religio Laici",' *Harvard Theological Review*, 54, 1961, pp. 207–21, and Thomas H. Fujimura, 'Dryden's "Religio Laici": An Anglican Poem', *PMLA*, 76, 1961, pp. 205–17.

[6] 'Apology for Raimond Sebond,' *The Essays of Michel de Montaigne*, trans. Jacob Zeitlin, Alfred Knopf, New York, 1935, Vol. 2, p. 233.

[7] Ibid.

put it, nearly as well as it is reputed to do, and that it must have depended upon some confirmatory argument in order to win acceptance.

The nature of this argument is not hard to discover. On three widely separated occasions, Dryden drew attention to what he chose to refer to as his 'scepticism'. If he had not done so, it is hard to imagine that the hypothesis we are considering would ever have been offered. But 'scepticism' is a highly ambiguous term which has more than one meaning in the seventeenth century, as anyone who cares to consult the *Oxford English Dictionary* can easily confirm. What the advocates of the theory that Dryden was a Pyrrhonist have done is to deny any ambiguity to the term by appealing not to the logical contexts in which Dryden uses the term, as we might expect them to do, but to his intellectual milieu. They have argued that philosophical scepticism, or Pyrrhonism, was a pervasive influence in the seventeenth century, that Dryden could scarcely have avoided coming in contact with it, and that his references to scepticism consequently can be taken only in this sense.

But to argue in this way is to proceed in the manner which R. S. Crane recently described when he referred to the method of those critics of Book IV of *Gulliver's Travels* who 'suppose that there is a kind of probative force in [one] preferred formula for [a] period which can confer, a priori, if not a unique at least a privileged relevance on one particular hypothesis about a given work of that period'.[8] To do so has meant, in this case, ignoring both the logical contexts of Dryden's remarks about his own scepticism and the possibility of there being other intellectual traditions in his own time which might better account for his use of this term.

To begin with Dryden's statements concerning his scepticism, there is a rather remarkable similarity about the contexts in which they appear. The first of these is a famous passage in his 'Defence of "An Essay of Dramatic Poesy" ' (1668), an answer to the charges which Dryden's brother-in-law, Sir Robert Howard, had levelled against the 'Essay' in the preface to *The Duke of Lerma*. Among other things, Howard had accused him of setting himself up as a legislator for the drama and of enacting rules which all playwrights were expected to obey, so that the 'Essay' is nothing less than an 'attempt to infringe the Liberty of Opinion by Rules' and an arrogant assumption of the right to 'dictate Lawes for *Dramatick Poesie*'.[9] Dryden replies:

> He is here pleased to charge me with being magisterial, as he has done in many other places of his preface. Therefore, in vindication of myself, I must crave leave to say that my whole discourse was sceptical, according to that way of reasoning which was used by

[8] 'The Houyhnhnms, the Yahoos, and the History of Ideas', *Reason and the Imagination: Studies in the History of Ideas 1600–1800*, ed. J. A. Mazzeo, Columbia University Press, New York, 1962, p. 240.

[9] 'To the Reader', *The Great Favourite, or, The Duke of Lerma*, London, 1668, sig. A4v.

Socrates, Plato, and all the Academics of old, which Tully and the best of the Ancients followed, and which is imitated by the modest inquisitions of the Royal Society. That it is so, not only the name will shew, which is *An Essay*, but the frame and composition of the work. You see it is a dialogue sustained by persons of several opinions, all of them left doubtful, to be determined by the readers in general.[10]

The term 'sceptical' here is being used to describe a 'way of reasoning', or mode of inquiry, applicable to a wide variety of philosophers, not a theory of knowledge with which several of them would have had no wish to be associated. It is a method of 'modest inquisition' which consists in investigating a question in an open and unbiased manner and in letting the reader make up his mind for himself.

The next time Dryden spoke of scepticism in connection with himself he was anticipating the same charge of being magisterial that Howard had levelled against him and answering it in advance. He begins the preface to 'Religio Laici' (1682) by admitting that

a POEM with so bold a Title, and a Name prefix'd, from which the handling of so serious a Subject wou'd not be expected, may reasonably oblige the Author, to say somewhat in defence both of himself, and of his undertaking. In the first place, if it be objected to me that being a *Layman*, I ought not to have concern'd my self with Speculations, which belong to the Profession of *Divinity* . . . I pretend not to make my self a Judge of Faith, in others, but onely to make a Confession of my own; I lay no unhallow'd hand upon the Ark; but wait on it, with the Reverence that becomes me at a distance. . . . Being naturally inclin'd to Scepticism in Philosophy, I have no reason to impose my Opinions, in a Subject which is above it: But whatever they are, I submit them with all reverence to my Mother Church.[11]

Howard had called him a dictator of laws for dramatic poesy; here Dryden makes sure that no one shall call him a judge of faith. Again his defence is a rather exaggerated modesty, the diffidence of one who is content to make a confession of his own faith without presuming to meddle with that of the reader. The words 'being naturally inclin'd to Scepticism in Philosophy' have often been quoted out of their context and, by an equation of 'Scepticism in Philosophy' with 'philosophical scepticism', have been treated as an admission on Dryden's part to Pyrrhonism. But to do this is to ignore the parallel elements in his sentence: 'Scepticism' is contrasted with 'to impose my Opinions', 'Philosophy' with 'a Subject which is above it', or theology. Dryden is simply offering the a fortiori argument that, as one who is instinctively diffident in matters inferior to faith, he is even less inclined to grow magisterial

[10] *Of Dramatic Poesy and Other Critical Essays*, ed. George Watson, J. M. Dent and Sons, London, 1962, Vol. 1, p. 123. (Hereafter referred to as *Essays*.)
[11] *The Poems of John Dryden*, ed. James Kinsley, Clarendon Press, Oxford, 1958, Vol. 1, p. 302. (Hereafter referred to as *Poems*.)

in a higher sphere and to become a judge of faith, where he possesses no special competence. Once again he is drawing our attention to his way of reasoning, not to his theory of knowledge.

Dryden's final allusion to his sceptical temperament occurs three years later in the 'Preface to *Sylvae*' (1685), where he is describing the 'distinguishing Character' of Lucretius, whom he had translated. This character emerges as just such a magisterial one as he had previously denied to be his own. Lucretius, Dryden writes, is remarkable for

> a certain kind of noble pride, and positive assertion of his Opinions. He is every where confident of his own reason, and assuming an absolute command not only over his vulgar Reader, but even his Patron *Memmius*. For he is always bidding him attend, as if he had the Rod over him; and using a Magisterial authority, while he instructs him. . . . he seems to disdain all manner of Replies, and is so confident of his cause, that he is before hand with his Antagonists; Urging for them, whatever he imagin'd they cou'd say, and leaving them as he supposes, without an objection for the future. All this too, with so much scorn and indignation, as if he were assur'd of the Triumph, before he enter'd into the Lists. . . . These are the considerations which I had of that Author, before I attempted to translate some parts of him. And accordingly I lay'd by my natural Diffidence and Scepticism for a while, to take up that Dogmatical way of his.[12]

The opposite of Dryden's own natural diffidence and scepticism, then, is a manner of inquiring into a subject, and a method of presenting one's conclusions, which he describes as positive assertion, magisterial authority, and a dogmatical way. It consists in a supreme confidence in one's own judgement, the putting forward of private opinions as indisputable truths, and an arrogant attempt to impose these views upon the reader. For such overconfidence, the only remedy is the modesty of the honest seeker after truth who welcomes discussion and stands ready to yield to better judgement, modifying his own conclusions accordingly.

I believe we must conclude that in none of these personal references to scepticism is Dryden alluding to a theory of knowledge. This is not to deny that Dryden knew the writings of Montaigne, admired him as an essayist, and could quote him on occasion—as has many another writer who did not share Montaigne's Pyrrhonism. Nor is it to deny that, having read widely among the classical authors and made the acquaintance of Diogenes Laertius and of Thomas Stanley's *History of Philosophy*, Dryden was perfectly familiar with the teachings of ancient scepticism under both its forms.[13] This is readily apparent from his

---

[12] Ibid., p. 395.

[13] ''Tis true that Diogenes Laertius, and our learned countryman Mr Stanley, have both written the lives of the philosophers; but we are more obliged to the various principles of their several sects than to any thing remarkable that they did for our entertainment' ('The Life of Lucian', *Essays*, Vol. 2, pp. 209–10).

lives of Plutarch and Lucian, where, in several passages which are simply paraphrases of the more learned commentators upon whom he is drawing, he describes the beliefs of the Pyrrhonists and of the New Academy as the doctrines of two ancient sects which claimed the allegiance of Lucian and Plutarch respectively.[14] But because of the historical and biographical context in which they appear, Dryden can assume that the terms 'Sceptic' and 'sect of Sceptics' which he introduces into the 'Lives' will be taken as referring to an ancient school of philosophy.[15] When, in an altogether different context, Dryden alludes to his own 'natural Diffidence and Scepticism' or 'sceptical way of reasoning', and contrasts this with a 'Magisterial' or 'Dogmatical' manner, he assumes the reader's familiarity with these terms in a quite separate sense. This latter conception of two modes of logical procedure, offered to the reader by means of two kinds of discourse, invites some sort of historical explanation, as does Dryden's assumption that the names of scepticism and dogmatism which he gives them will be readily understood.

I think we can see what such a historical explanation would require. It would have to find, not a tradition of attacking the reliability of reason and the senses, but a habit of presenting two opposite ways of reasoning, one of which is recommended, under the name of scepticism, as a kind of modesty and diffidence, while the other is condemned, under some such name as dogmatism, as a kind of positiveness of opinion. And this historical explanation would have to show, not simply that this tradition was a pervasive influence in the seventeenth century, or part of the intellectual climate of that age which the English presumably shared with the French, but that it was a body of opinion with which Englishmen in the 1660s and 1670s were readily familiar and which Dryden could take for granted in his own rather casual references to scepticism in these years. It would require, in other words, a search, not for world pictures or intellectual milieus, but for particular contexts.

I should like to suggest that such a body of opinion can be discovered in some of those books which began to appear at about the time the

[14] See ibid., p. 210, and 'The Life of Plutarch', *Works*, Vol. 17, pp. 31–2. The late E. N. Hooker assumed that in the latter passage Dryden undertook to describe a position which he shared with Plutarch. He therefore concluded that Dryden professed the modified scepticism of the New Academy (see 'Dryden and the Atoms of Epicurus', *ELH*, 24, 1957, p. 184). George Watson, however, has excluded the passage from his edition of Dryden's criticism on the grounds that it is simply a recasting of 'material explicitly translated or adapted from continental treatises and commentaries' (*Essays*, Vol. 1, p. xvii), and A. E. Wallace Maurer has shown that Dryden is indebted to Jean Ruault for the entire passage (see 'Dryden and Pyrrhonism', *Notes and Queries*, 202, 1957, pp. 251–2).

[15] In both lives, Dryden reserves the term 'Sceptic' for a member of the Pyrrhonist sect. His name for one who professes the scepticism of the New Academy is 'an Academic, that is, half Platonist, half Sceptic' ('The Life of Plutarch', *Works*, Vol. 17, p. 72). This obviously contradicts Hooker's thesis that Dryden's references to his own scepticism are intended as synonyms for Academic probabilism.

Royal Society was founded and which sought to publicize the activities of that group or actually to put into effect some part of its programme. One of the matters which receives special emphasis in these books is the method of reasoning which the members of the Royal Society use, and the manner in which they offer the results of this reasoning to others. Joseph Glanvill described their procedure in *Plus Ultra* as one which

> renders them *wary* and *modest*, *diffident* of the *certainty* of their *Conceptions*, and averse to the *boldness* of *peremptory asserting*. So that the *Philosopher thinks much*, and *examines* many things, separates the *Certainties* from the *Plausibilities*, *that* which is *presumed* from *that* which is *prov'd*, the *Images* of *Sense*, *Phansie*, and *Education*, from the *Dictates* of *genuine* and *impartial Reason*. This he doth before he *Assents* or *Denies*; and *then* he takes with him also a Sense of his own *Fallibility* and *Defects*, and never concludes but upon resolution to alter his mind upon contrary evidence. Thus he conceives *warily*, and he speaks with as much *caution* and *reserve*, in the humble Forms of *So I think*, and *In my opinion*, and *Perhaps 'tis so*—with great [deference] to *opposite* Perswasion, candour to *dissenters*, and *calmness* in *contradictions*, with *readiness* and *desire* to *learn*, and great delight in the Discoveries of Truth, and Detections of his *own* Mistakes.[16]

This was published in 1668, the very year in which Dryden was describing his own way of reasoning in the 'Essay' in closely similar terms, and likening it to 'the modest inquisitions of the Royal Society'. The opposite of such a way of reasoning, according to the members of the Royal Society, was that of the ancients, especially Aristotle, which consisted in a haughty confidence in one's own opinions and an arrogant attempt to impose them upon others. The most common term for this was dogmatism, and under this name it was frequently denounced by the advocates of the new philosophy. They had several names for their own way of reasoning, and one of these was scepticism.

A particularly striking parallel to Dryden's habit of contrasting dogmatism and scepticism as two opposite ways of reasoning is offered by Glanvill's earliest book. This popular work has as its subject the two ways of reasoning and of offering opinions which we are concerned with. It undertakes to condemn the ancient practice of laying down the law of nature as a thing already understood and ratified, and to advocate in its place a more diffident form of inquiry. When the book appeared the first time, in 1661, Glanvill chose a title which would stress the method he condemned, and he called his discourse *The Vanity of Dogmatizing*. But when he reissued the book in a new form in 1665, three years before Dryden's 'Defence of "An Essay of Dramatic Poesy",' he decided to give a more positive emphasis to the title, and he renamed it *Scepsis Scientifica*, in reference to the method espoused in the book. It

16 *Plus Ultra*, London, 1668, pp. 146–7.

was dedicated this time to the Royal Society, because, Glanvill wrote, 'regarding Your *Society* as the strongest *Argument* to perswade a *modest* and *reserved diffidence* in opinions, I took the boldness to borrow that deservedly celebrated *name*, for an *evidence* to my Subject'.[17] With this idea in mind, Glanvill proceeded in his book to urge his readers to adopt 'the *Scepticism* which consists in *Freedome* of *inquiry*', and to assure them that '*Scepticism*, that's the only way to *Science*'.[18] Nevertheless, Glanvill was careful to point out that if he was sceptical, he was no Pyrrhonist, and that in advocating modesty, diffidence, and freedom of inquiry under the name of scepticism he was far from 'endeavouring to discourage *Philosophical* enquiries, by introducing a *despair* of *Science*' in the manner of the ancient Sceptics. He went on to declare firmly: 'I desire it may be taken notice of once for all then, that I have nought to do with that shuffling Sect, that love to doubt eternally, and to question all things. My profession is *freedom* of *enquiry*, and I own no more *Scepticism* then what is concluded in the *Motto* which the ROYAL SOCIETY have now adopted for theirs, NULLIUS IN VERBA [on the word of no one].'[19]

Robert Boyle, the most prominent member of the Royal Society during its early years, placed a similar stress upon modesty and diffidence and upon freedom of inquiry; he too sometimes described his method as 'sceptical'. In one of his earliest books, *Certain Physiological Essays* (1661), he considered it a matter for special remark 'that in almost every one of the following essays I should speak so doubtingly, and use so often, *perhaps, it seems, it is not improbable*, and such other expressions, as argue a diffidence of the truth of the opinions I incline to, and that I should be so shy of laying down principles, and sometimes of so much as venturing at explications'.[20] His emphasis here upon modesty of expression is complemented by the importance he gives to freedom of inquiry in another of his early books, also published in 1661. *The Sceptical Chymist, or, Chymico-Physical Doubts and Paradoxes* is, like Dryden's 'Essay of Dramatic Poesy', a 'dialogue sustained by persons of several opinions', one of Boyle's favourite literary forms. In this dialogue, the sceptical chemist of the title, representing Boyle's own point of view, proposes doubts concerning the currently accepted alchemical theories. But like Glanvill, Boyle is careful to point out that it is possible to be sceptical without sharing the theory of knowledge of the ancient Sceptics.

For though sometimes I have had occasion to discourse like a Sceptick, yet I am far from being one of that sect; which I take to have been little less prejudicial to natural philosophy than to divinity itself.

[17] 'To the Royal Society', *Scepsis Scientifica*, London, 1665, sig. A4.
[18] Ibid., p. 56, and 'Sciri tuum nihil est', ibid., p. 12.
[19] 'Sciri tuum nihil est', ibid., p. 3.
[20] *Certain Physiological Essays, The Works of the Hon. Robert Boyle*, ed. Thomas Birch, 2nd edn, London, 1772, Vol. 1, p. 307.

F

I do not with the true Scepticks propose doubts to persuade men, that all things are doubtful and will ever remain so (at least) to human understandings; but I propose doubts not only with design, but with hope, of being at length freed from them by the attainment of undoubted truth; which I seek, that I may find it; though if I miss of it in one opinion, I proceed to search after it in the opposite, or in any other where it seems more likely I should meet with it.[21]

It is this emphasis upon doubts (*scepses*) that led the members of the Royal Society to apply to their own procedure the terms 'sceptical' and 'scepticism' also adopted by the Pyrrhonists.[22] But as Boyle, Glanvill and Thomas Sprat in his *History of the Royal Society* (1667) all make clear, there is an enormous difference between themselves and the Pyrrhonists in the use which they make of doubts.[23] The Pyrrhonists, because of their theory of knowledge, 'love to doubt eternally', and 'propose doubts to persuade men that all things are doubtful'. The doubts proposed by the members of the Royal Society, on the other hand, are merely temporary, the initial ingredients of a method of procedure which will lead ultimately to 'the attainment of undoubted truth'.

This method of preliminary doubt was inherited from Bacon, as the members of the Royal Society frequently stressed.[24] It is a conception which Bacon expressed in an oft-quoted remark in *The Advancement of Learning*: 'If a man will begin with certainties, he shall end in doubts; but if he will be content to begin with doubts, he shall end in certainties.'[25] In urging this method of temporary doubt, and attacking those who 'render sciences dogmatic and magisterial' in the manner of Aristotle, who 'laid down the law on all points', Bacon is as careful as his successors later in the century to distinguish the doubts he recommends from those of the Pyrrhonists.[26] In one of many such passages which abound in his works, he writes:

[21] Appendix to 'The Sceptical Chymist', ibid., p. 591. This appendix was added to the second edition of 1679.

[22] Like Dryden (see note 15 above), the other members of the Royal Society, when referring to the ancient sceptical sects, reserved the term 'Sceptics' for the Pyrrhonists and designated the sceptics of the New Academy by the name of 'Academics'. See Henry Oldenburg's practice in the *Philosophical Transactions*, Vol. 7, 1672, p. 5081, and Vol. 11, 1676, p. 791. According to Richard H. Popkin, this was the common practice of most writers of the sixteenth and seventeenth centuries. See *The History of Scepticism from Erasmus to Descartes*, Van Gorcum, Assen, The Netherlands, 1960, pp. xii–xiii.

[23] For an extended discussion of this difference, see Thomas Sprat, *The History of the Royal Society*, London, 1667, pp. 101, 106–8.

[24] The Royal Society's debt to Bacon in this and other respects is thoroughly discussed by Richard Foster Jones in *Ancients and Moderns*, Washington University Press, St. Louis, 1936.

[25] 'The Advancement of Learning', in *The Works of Francis Bacon*, ed. J. Spedding, R. L. Ellis, and D. D. Heath, Longman and Co., London, 1857–74, Vol. 3, p. 293.

[26] 'Novum Organum', in ibid., Vol. 4, p. 69.

It will also be thought that by forbidding men to pronounce and to set down principles as established until they have duly arrived through the intermediate steps at the highest generalities, I maintain a sort of suspension of the judgement, and bring it to what the Greeks call *Acatalepsia*,—a denial of the capacity of the mind to comprehend truth. But in reality that which I mediate and propound is not *Acatalepsia*, but *Eucatalepsia*; not denial of the capacity to understand, but provision for understanding truly; for I do not take away authority from the senses, but supply them with helps; I do not slight the understanding, but govern it.[27]

It is this conception of doubt as a temporary mental discipline, the preliminary stage in every inquiry which must ultimately lead to certitude, that distinguishes the new scientists from the Pyrrhonists. The scepticism of the Royal Society is an essential ingredient, not of a theory of knowledge, but of a scientific method; yet it is squarely based upon an optimistic epistemology which denies and contradicts the tenets of philosophical scepticism.[28]

In the passages I have quoted, Boyle and Glanvill describe the scepticism of the Royal Society sometimes as modesty and diffidence, sometimes as freedom of inquiry. Both characteristics are derived from the importance which they attach to doubt, and therefore both are properly described as 'sceptical'. Freedom of inquiry, which the members of the Royal Society had learned from Bacon to claim as their right, consisted in taking *Nullius in Verba* as their motto and questioning the opinions of the ancients. Their first doubts, then, concerned the scientific principles inherited from the past, and, as Sprat wrote, 'out of a just disdain, that the *Antients* should still possess a Tyranny over our Judgements, [they] began first to put off the reverence that men had born to their memories'.[29] But that which rendered these inherited principles dubious in their eyes was the fact that the ancients themselves had lacked a capacity for self-doubt. 'The greatest occasion of

[27] Ibid., pp. 111–12. Other passages in the 'Novum Organum' which stress the differences between the Baconian method of doubt and philosophical scepticism occur on pp. 39, 53, and 68–9. See also 'The Advancement of Learning', in ibid., Vol. 3, p. 293, and 'Instauratio Magna', ibid., Vol. 4, p. 32.

[28] See the illuminating discussion by Sir Karl Popper of the contrast between the 'optimistic epistemology' underlying the Baconian and Cartesian methods of doubt and the 'pessimistic epistemology' of Montaigne and the other philosophical sceptics in *Conjectures and Refutations*, Routledge and Kegan Paul, London, 1963, pp. 3–30. For the survival of this optimistic epistemology among later seventeenth-century scientists before Newton, see Ralph M. Blake, 'Natural Science in the Renaissance', *Theories of Scientific Method : The Renaissance through the Nineteenth Century*, ed. Edward H. Madden, University of Washington Press, Seattle, 1960, pp. 3–21; the same author's 'Isaac Newton and the Hypothetico-Deductive Method', ibid., pp. 119–43; and Edward Grant, 'Hypotheses in Late Medieval and Early Modern Science', *Daedalus*, 91, 1962, pp. 599–616.

[29] *History of the Royal Society*, p. 29.

our dissenting from the *Greek Philosophers*, and especially from *Aristotle*', according to Sprat, 'was, that they made too much hast to seise on the prize, before they were at the end of the Race: that they fix'd, and determin'd their judgements, on general conclusions too soon, and so could not afterwards alter them, by any new appearances, which might represent themselves'.[30] Their very dogmatism had made them immune to that self-criticism which is essential to every seeker after truth.

It was not enough, therefore, simply to doubt the teachings of the ancients. The members of the Royal Society must doubt their own conclusions and cultivate a diffidence of opinion, striving to overcome that 'impatience of doubt, and haste to assertion without due and mature suspension of judgement' which Bacon had condemned, but to which all men unfortunately are subject.[31] 'They love not a long and a tedious doubting', Sprat remarked, 'though it brings them at last to a real certainty: but they choose rather to conclude presently, then to be long in suspence, though to better purpose'.[32] Modesty and diffidence, as pursued by the members of the Royal Society, represent a deliberate attempt to overcome this natural tendency and to encourage the same scepticism toward their own efforts as they directed toward those of their predecessors. 'Wherever [the reader] finds that I have ventur'd at any small Conjectures, at the causes of the things that I have observed', another prominent member of the Society warned in 1665, 'I beseech him to look upon them only as *doubtful Problems*, and *uncertain ghesses*, and not as unquestionable Conclusions, or matters of unconfutable Science; I have produced nothing here, with intent to bind his understanding to an *implicit* consent'.[33] If scepticism was an antidote for the dogmatism of the ancients, it was also a preservative against the same malady among the moderns.

These two characteristics, then, of freedom of inquiry and of modesty and diffidence were the essential ingredients of that method of investigation which was given the name of 'scepticism' in the mid-seventeenth century. It was these same two characteristics which Glanvill, in his essay 'Of Scepticism and Certainty' (1676), selected as justifying the use of the term 'scepticism' in connection with the Royal Society. The 'modern free philosophers', he wrote, can be described as 'sceptical' because (1) they 'dare dissent from the *Aristotelian* Doctrines, and will not slavishly subscribe [to] all the Tenents of that *Dictator* in *Philosophy*'; and (2) they 'proceed with wariness and circumspection without too much forwardness in establishing Maxims, and positive Doctrines'.[34]

---

[30] Ibid., p. 30. For a similar complaint against the ancients' lack of diffidence, see Boyle, 'Certain Physiological Essays', *Works*, Vol. 1, p. 302.

[31] 'The Advancement of Learning', in *Works of Francis Bacon*, Vol. 3, p. 293.

[32] *History of the Royal Society*, p. 32.

[33] Robert Hooke, *Micrographia*, London, 1665, sig. bl.

[34] 'Of Scepticism and Certainty', *Essays on Several Important Subjects in Philosophy and Religion*, London, 1676, pp. 43–5.

If Dryden's 'way of reasoning' in his 'Essay of Dramatic Poesy' was in imitation of 'the modest inquisitions of the Royal Society', his description of the 'Essay' as a 'sceptical discourse' was appropriate and accurate. . . .

Unquestionably, scepticism is an important part of Dryden's characteristic thought. But it is a very different matter from the Pyrrhonism with which it has been so long identified. Indeed, it is in certain important respects the very opposite. Far from being a sign of Dryden's 'anti-rationalism', his scepticism is a confident affirmation of the powers of human reason. When unexamined opinion is accepted as a substitute for honest investigation, Dryden believed, reason is betrayed and truth made captive. But when the pursuit of knowledge is 'rightly and generally cultivated', errors will be detected and truth prevail. In his repeated expression of this hopeful belief, Dryden is not the least among the '*Assertors* of free Reason's claim'.

From Chapter 1 of *Contexts of Dryden's Thought*, Chicago, 1968, pp. 1–31 (1–15, 31).

Dryden's Ceremonial Hero

Because so many poems of the Restoration and early eighteenth century are occasional, it is easy to believe one understands them when their literary allusions are noted and the local references are placed in a historical or philosophical context. This is especially true of the early poems of Dryden, addressed to particular persons and dealing with contemporary subjects. And because Dryden's first political and religious shifts occur during his early poetic career, his poems during this period have often been pointed to as literary hackwork and as evidence that the author was a time-server. While the Romantic misconceptions about Dryden are no longer current, students and critics alike still too often assume that he has no sustained poetic stance, no persistent way of looking at art and the world that transcends the immediate moment. Only recently has attention been drawn to the continuity in his poetic methods and the recurrence of particular themes in his poetry.[1] I would like to point out Dryden's use of a poetic character, prominent in his early verse and returned to in his mature poetry, which reveals consistency in his artistic techniques and helps define certain habits of his mind.

With few exceptions Dryden's first poems are addressed to national heroes who, praised by means of similar techniques, are transformed into a single poetic character that has a remarkably similar function in the poems. Even though the separate poems concern themselves with specific persons and contemporary events, the figure of the hero portrayed is consistent and uniform. After examining Dryden's recurring theme, his management of historical material, and the techniques by which the hero is extolled, one can see that Cromwell, Charles II, James, Clarendon, Charleton, and even Hastings are pictured as changing faces of a single figure, which because of his poetic function can be called the ceremonial hero.

Although Dryden inherited a concept of the hero from the Renaissance and techniques for praising great men from earlier poets of the seventeenth century,[2] he constructs a central figure distinguished in its

---

[1] Some of the more important studies are Arthur W. Hoffman, *John Dryden's Imagery*, Gainesville, Fla., 1962; John Winterbottom, 'The Development of the Hero in Dryden's Tragedies', *JEGP*, 52, 1953, pp. 161–73; Alan Roper, *Dryden's Poetic Kingdoms*, London, 1965; Earl W. Miner, 'Some Characteristics of Dryden's Use of Metaphor', *SEL*, 2, 1962, pp. 309–20.

[2] Ruth Nevo, *The Dial of Virtue*, Princeton, 1963, traces developments in ideas and techniques of political poems in the seventeenth century. As this

uniting disparate qualities from the heroic traditions with the attributes of leadership needed in the existing social order, and he does so in a manner that blends metaphysical imagery with Augustan wit. Contemporary history had shown the instability of the political system and the need for leaders dedicated to the preservation of order, yet historical events had not destroyed for Dryden the ideal of heroism inherited from the Elizabethans; Dryden infuses the epic qualities of the hero with social and religious significance. The distance between the hero and the people remains, but what is of interest to Dryden are the moments when that distance is bridged. Dryden's poems transform public events into ritualistic celebrations of the union of the hero and the nation as they move toward spiritual and patriotic goals; thus, the principal figure in them can properly be termed ceremonial.

I

Dryden's early poems—no matter to whom they are addressed—have more or less the same structure. Historical facts form a foundation or framework for the poem, yet the events are ordered so that there is a similar theme in each poem, which is some variation on the idea of redemption—the transition from chaos to order, sin to forgiveness, or despair to hope; the hero, the living representative of the spiritual processes acting in the world, unites the theme and situation. Such a pattern allows the poem to end usually with a prophecy of the future glory of England.

The body of the poems begins—at times after an introductory section—by ordering events to illustrate the need for change—the first step in advancing the theme of the return of order—or by superimposing on contemporary events a literary fable that suggests the theme. England in 'Astraea Redux' is pictured as separated from the 'general Peace', and recent history is compared to the chaotic periods when Jove was forced to fly 'from his own Heaven' and when the Cyclops had 'lawless salvage Libertie'. The Flood is the metaphor in 'To His Sacred Maiesty' by which contemporary history is understood and judged. The contrasts between the present and past in poems immediately after the Restoration are, of course, easy and obvious. Yet a similar contrast occurs in 'Heroique Stanza's' when Dryden pictures the disorder prior to Cromwell's ascendency.

> Our former Chiefs like sticklers of the Warre
> First sought t' inflame the Parties, then to poise;
> The quarrell lov'd, but did the cause abhorre,
> And did not strike to hurt but make a noise.
>
> (lines 41–4)

paper will demonstrate, I find Professor Nevo's discussion of Dryden's early political poems as examples of the 'baroque heroic' an inadequate, although not always inappropriate, context for understanding the poems.

And in 'To Dr Charleton' the poet arranges discoveries in science to show the freeing of the mind from 'The longest Tyranny that ever sway'd'. In this poem when either the restoration of science or of a strong monarchy is being praised, the principal concern—as in the overtly political poems—is the process taking place, the movement from ignorance to knowledge, of anarchy to order. And the processes end with the union of a throne and a temple, the earthly and divine, conforming to the theme of the other poems addressed to great men.

The middle sections of the poems announce the return of order by defining the figure and the function of the hero, whose career reflects the spiritual and historical process. But the hero is not pictured in isolation; even though this section concentrates on the hero's individual accomplishments and attributes, it also suggests his relationship to the general social order. In 'To My Lord Chancellor' virtues of the hero are shown to parallel the general task of the state, the dispensing of justice and mercy, and in 'To His Sacred Maiesty' the hero is called upon to be both Caesar and father to the people. The allusions in 'Astraea Redux' to Moses, Adam, Christ, and Aeneas suggest that the hero is closely allied to a culture and bears in some way its past guilt and hardships. When Charles arrives in England, seasonal changes are stressed: 'you renew'd the expiring Pomp of *May!*'; Charles's star which 'shone out so bright' and now 'its potent Fires renew' has gone through a diminution that could recur. The section forces the reader to think of process and change, indicating the precarious relationship of the people and king, before England's glory is prophesied, a future dependent on the mutual interdependence of the king and people.

The ultimate purpose of the early poems is revealed by their conclusions which chiefly prophesy, not the continuing grandeur of the hero, but the glory of England. In 'To His Sacred Maiesty' the hero's general function is the drying of the 'false and slipp'ry ground' left by the Flood, and the hero becomes, as the poem progresses, a nature-god forgiving the past 'life and sin' and turning the dead land into a garden paradise. Yet the conclusion of the poem, while concentrating on the hero, demonstrates that the future of England and the theme of regeneration are the poet's primary concerns. Dryden pictures the king pursuing pleasures—building a canal from St James's Park to the Thames—congruous with his duties as defender of the seas. The water lane, while incidentally giving the sea a 'Royal bed', is primarily a port through which will come a Queen 'from whose chast womb . . . The souls of Kings unborn for bodies wait'. And the four lines foretelling happiness are:

Thus from your Royal Oke, like *Jove's* of old,
Are answers sought, and destinies fore-told:
Propitious Oracles are beg'd with vows,
And Crowns that grow upon the sacred boughs.

(lines 129–32)

While Charles's past life and the devices built for the coronation are here referred to, the lines are directly related to the references to the king's plans to marry; the oak and boughs have significance as symbols of the king's priestly powers, yet also allude to his role as begetter of future kings of England. Actions of the hero are both private and public since they reflect his will but affect all members of the realm. The poem ends, not looking forward to the glory of the hero, but requesting that the king act so that his subjects 'may possesse / With their own peace their Childrens happinesse'.

The structure and conclusion of 'To Dr Charleton' conform to those of Dryden's political poems. In his important article on the poem Professor Wasserman demonstrates that '. . . the recent turn of political events constituted for Dryden an essential ordinance that gives shape and meaning to other matters . . .'.[3] Yet in the poem other matters, the rise of English science and the international fame of English men of genius, are also means for affirming the future political stability. This should suggest that while the state was for Dryden the most obvious object or symbol in which man can read nature, other forces or systems were following the same patterns that were discernible in the political makeup of society. In 'To Sir Robert Howard' Dryden sees in art the same growth to order and stability occurring in government. In 'To Dr Charleton' the growth of truth, or the rise of the Royal Society, or specifically the acquisition of knowledge about Stonehenge, repeats a process—the theme of most of Dryden's early poems—that illustrates England's progress towards greatness.

While the early poems are structured to reveal the process of re-generation, the figure of the hero dominates them. The man addressed in the poem is both a person and a representative figure that takes part in the spiritual and historical processes suggested by the theme. Just as fables and allusions from the classical and Christian traditions are superimposed on contemporary history to reveal the significance of the temporal process, so they are also employed to transform a living man into an idealized figure. Recent history tempers the allusions and stories, while they give history a new perspective. Charles II is introduced into 'Astraea Redux' as a suffering hero:

How Great were then Our *Charles* his Woes, who thus
Was forc'd to suffer for Himself and us!
He toss'd by Fate, and hurried up and down,
Heir to his Fathers Sorrows, with his Crown.

(lines 49–52)

While the allusions suggest that Charles is more than a historical personage, is in fact a cultural hero, the historical basis of the poem

[3] Earl R. Wasserman, 'Dryden's Epistle to Charleton', *JEGP*, 55, 1956, pp. 201–12.

makes it impossible to identify him completely with either Christ or Aeneas. The hero is named so that his suffering remains only a type of Christ's, and since Charles's father possessed a crown as well as being tossed by fate, the image of Aeneas does not replace the actual king of England whose father was killed by the rebellious forces denounced a few lines earlier. The man and his symbolic function are balanced; the hero is both an individual and a representative figure.

To define the peculiar qualities of his hero, Dryden unites ideals from the separate heroic traditions. The hero possesses active and passive virtues, inherent in both the Christian and Roman traditions but not usually so, almost quantitatively, balanced as in Dryden's portraits. Wit and imagery unite or keep in tension logically contrary ideas. The courage and virtue practised in pursuit of destiny are placed alongside the sorrows and wounds inflicted by fate; the imperial daring that conquers the world is tempered by a Stoic recognition of the insignificance of man in general nature. In 'Astraea Redux' the contemplative and active virtues of the classical world result in a thoughtfully controlled government.

> Inur'd to suffer ere he came to raigne
> No rash procedure will his actions stain.
> To bus'ness ripened by digestive thought
> His future rule is into Method brought.   (lines 87–90)

Christianity provides, however, the grander, the more sublime antitheses; the passivity that conquers nature, the suffering that storms heaven. The humble prayer of the hero takes heaven by force.

> Yet as he knew his blessings worth, took care
> That we should know it by repeated pray'r;
> Which storm'd the skies and ravish'd *Charles* from thence
> As Heav'n it self is took by violence.   (lines 141–4)

In 'To His Sacred Maiesty' Dryden unites the Roman and Christian ideas of the hero by asking that Charles assume the functions of Caesar and of father. Yet the only actions of Charles typifying those of Caesar, the secular head of state, are the quieting of rebellious sects and promoting religious toleration. And while alluding to the command, 'Render unto Caesar . . .', in the couplet, 'You for their Umpire and their Synod take,/And their appeal alone to *Caesar* make', Dryden heals the traditional breach between the duties owed to the state and to God.

The contrary virtues of the hero, which are shown in the poems to be complementary, are not assigned to one historical person; in 'Astraea Redux' such qualities are possessed by Charles; in 'Heroique Stanza's', by Cromwell. In the earlier poem which reviews the forging of an empire the 'emperor' is first pictured as motionless and serene. And before tracing Cromwell's actions, Dryden praises his stable, contemplative nature: 'He, private, mark'd the faults of others sway,/And set as *Sea-mark's* for himself to shun', 'Peace was the Prize of all his toyles and care,/Which Warre had banisht and did now restore'. His conquests end in peace; the image of his great activities becomes one of rest and stability.

> He fought secure of fortune as of fame,
> Till by new *maps* the Island might be shown,
> Of Conquests which he strew'd where e're he came
> Thick as the *Galaxy* with starr's is sown. (lines 53–6)

Dryden's uniting of seemingly contradictory virtues of the hero is made easier in 'To My Lord Chancellor' since he praises two men, each of whom may represent separate aspects of the complex hero. Because of the actual governmental tasks of the two men, one, the king, may be pictured as the hero removed from mundane strife, while the other, the chancellor, can fulfil in time and space the function of the hero; Clarendon is the 'Channel' through whom flows the 'vital influence' of 'The Nations soul (our Monarch)'. Images suggest the differing natures and functions of the two forces, yet also picture the necessity for each as complements to one another.

> In open prospect nothing bounds our eye
> Until the Earth seems joyn'd unto the sky:
> So in this Hemisphaer our utmost view
> Is only bounded by our King and you:
> Our sight is limited where you are joyn'd
> And beyond that no farther Heav'n can find.
> So well your Vertues do with his agree
> That though your Orbs of different greatness be,
> Yet both are for each others use dispos'd,
> His to inclose, and yours to be inclos'd. (lines 31–40)

These complementary attributes are united in the figure of the single hero in the other panegyrics.

While wit and allusions are important in defining the figure of the hero, astronomical imagery is perhaps more persistently and functionally employed. When Dryden praises Cromwell, the image of the circle both suggests the heavenly import of the hero's destiny and summarizes and sets in order his past actions. After establishing political stability in England. Cromwell extends his power outwardly in successive waves to the conquests of Ireland and Scotland, peace with Holland, influence over France and Spain, and curbing of 'Proud Rome'. As Cromwell's actions move in expanding circles, so his fame is 'truely Circular', 'For in a round what order can be shew'd,/Where all the parts so *equall perfect* are?'.

The same image dominates the conclusion of 'Astraea Redux';
Charles's empire, compared to the sun and time, expands in concentric
circles absorbing all in its path.

> Abroad your Empire shall no Limits know,
> But like the Sea in boundless Circles flow.
> Your much lov'd Fleet shall with a wide Command
> Besiege the petty Monarchs of the Land:
> And as Old Time his Off-spring swallow'd down
> Our Ocean in its depths all Seas shall drown.
>
> (lines 298–303)

Since the image of the circle suggests order and completion, it is parti-
cularly appropriate to prophecies of stability and beatitude, based on the
figure of the hero. The apostrophe to the hero concluding the poem
continues the balancing of action and submission; the 'factious Souls'
are reclaimed partly by 'your Edicts', but more importantly by 'your
Life and Blest Example'. And the action of Charles is circular, never
ending, recalling the allusions to time and the sea: 'Oh happy Prince
whom Heav'n hath taught the way/By paying Vowes, to have more
Vowes to pay!'.

Besides its denotation of perfection and completion, the circle can be
the principal image in Dryden's panegyrics because it so aptly objectifies
his vision of the state and society as the gathering into a whole of dis-
parate or separate parts: 'For in a round what order can be shew'd,/
Where all the parts so *equall perfect* are?'. After Frye, its appropriate-
ness in panegyrics to a hero which have a theme of regeneration need
not be laboured. Yet in the conclusion of 'To My Lord Chancellor' new
figures are adopted, retaining the traditional connotations of perfection,
stability, and divine influence, but expanding to include the more
complex ideas that the state as a subject demanded. From a baldly
melodramatic picture of Fortune's wheel stopped after the impossible
effort to keep pace with Clarendon's actions, the poet moves to a picture
of the earthly paradise, a visualization of the theme. While the image of
Clarendon as a mountain 'In these happy Isles' may be questioned on
the grounds of taste, Dryden's shift to the idyllic and natural is consis-
tent with his eclectic methods of magnifying the hero and his wish to
exploit the image of the circle.

Although it would be presumptuous to analyse the last lines when Dr
Johnson did not think himself 'obliged to tell the meaning', it can be
said that Dryden continues to bring to harmony supposedly contrary
facts, first by wit and then by imagery.

> Yet unimpair'd with labours or with time
> Your age but seems to a new youth to climb.
> Thus Heav'nly bodies do our time beget;
> And measure Change, but share no part of it.

And still it shall without a weight increase,
Like this New-year, whose motions never cease;
For since the glorious Course you have begun
Is led by CHARLS, as that is by the Sun,
It must both weightlesse and immortal prove,
Because the Center of it is above.   (lines 147–56)

Youth—age, change—timelessness, weight—weightlessness, a birth-day—immortality, all are yoked together as the two forces ruling England find their metaphorical centre in heaven. From a mythological emblem and from a natural paradise, the figure of the circle, having gained body in addition to shape, reappears finally as the sun, the most familiar, yet most significant, object from which it draws its meta-phorical power.

II

Dryden successfully employs the ceremonial hero as a poetic device only in the years 1659–63. During this time one political ruler died, others began their careers, and several important literary or scientific events occurred. All of these subjects could be celebrated in poems structured to show the increasing power and glory of England; the theme of the poems seemed actually to be working in the historical present. Yet the picturing of a ceremonial hero is, at least, attempted in Dryden's first poem, and the poet returns to this hero in his later verse. But in these other poems Dryden never successfully uses the figure, either because of poetic ineptness in one case or because of intellectual misgivings about the role of such a hero in society.

That Dryden is primarily interested in delineating the figure of a hero, not simply in praising contemporary governmental officials, is proven by his use of techniques in his first poem that recur whenever he addresses important personages in his early verse. The figure is constant while the subjects change. 'On the Death of Hastings' fails because of the substantive disparity between the actual facts—the historical material—and the figure being defined by the images and allusions; the subject was not personally or institutionally important enough to be presented as a hero, and the poet did not overcome the difficulty by generalizing, making representative, the life of Hastings as he later did so well with Anne Killigrew. No linguistic accomplishments of Hastings would permit him to be bluntly described as: 'Then Whom, Great *Alexander* may seem Less;/Who conquer'd Men, but not their Languages' (lines 17–18). The following metaphors, inherited from an earlier age, seek to transform the boy into the hero Dryden was later to celebrate by means of similar figures.

His Body was an Orb, his sublime Soul
Did move on Vertue's and on Learnings's Pole:

Whose Reg'lar Motions better to our view,
Then *Archimedes* Sphere, the Heavens did shew. . . .
Heav'ns Gifts, which do, like falling Stars, appear
Scatter'd in Others; all, as in their Sphear,
Were fix'd and conglobate in 's Soul; and thence
Shone th'row his Body, with sweet Influence.
(lines 27–30, 33–6)

The diction and imagery here will soon be applied with greater variety
of meaning, and because of the function of the men in society, with
greater significance, to Cromwell, Charles II, and Clarendon (similar
images also describe the fame of the scientists in 'To Dr Charleton').
The conceit, now notorious, describing Hastings's illness, is not a
technical ornament displaying the young poet's inventiveness, but
continuing the astronomical allusions, reinforces the concept of the
hero, here inappropriate, that Dryden has been defining.

And it is useful to look at Dryden's two public poems written after
1663—'Annus Mirabilis' and 'Absalom and Achitophel'—with the
earlier ones in mind. While the later poems are generically different
from the others, they do arrange history to demonstrate the return to
order, and they have a national figure as hero. One important difference
between the two sets of poems is the relationship of the hero to the
historical material presented in the poems. In the early group the central
figure is pictured as a hero, a man with a distinct and peculiar destiny.
Yet his function is that of a servant, a regenerative force in the nation,
a man who acts only as a part of a larger whole. The potential conflict
between figure and function never occurred in the early poems because
they celebrated ritualistically either the beginning or end of some
important aspect of the life of the hero. In the two later poems the hero
is in the midst of action; the poet pictures him only as he functions in
society, with the result that the figure of a hero with a separate destiny
is blurred. It should be noted that such a shift of emphasis is not
required by the change in genre. Society, not the hero, is now of chief
importance to Dryden. This fact helps explain why the conclusions of
both poems are weak, and that of the later poem, unconvincing;
Dryden gives the curtain speeches to a figure who throughout the
poems, while often talked about, is only a participant, not a controller
of action.

Throughout 'Annus Mirabilis', the king, as he decides on war, names
the commanders, supervises the repairs, attempts to control the fire,
and then prays for its end, obviously subjects his will to the good of the
nation; he rules by 'consensus'. His prayer, the climax of the poem,
dramatizes his position. Seeking nothing for himself, Charles asks only
for a stable government, and describes his past functions as binder of
the 'bruises of a Civil War' and a preserver of 'wasting bloud'. There is
magnanimity, yet it is achieved by the king's humility and selflessness.
While contrition is appropriate in a prayer, the passive elements in the

hero's character, balanced in previous poems by an active will, dominate the presentation of him in this poem.

The same is true in 'Absalom and Achitophel'. The king at the end of the poem affirms the presence of civil order by joining constitutional power with his own simplicity and sincerity, his qualities in 'Annus Mirabilis', and his speech contrasts sharply with the clever, witty speeches of Achitophel. (Wit in this poem is used almost exclusively to damn the rebels.) While the union of power and mercy grew out of the attributes of the hero in 'To My Lord Chancellor', in 'Absalom and Achitophel' it is assumed to be inherent in the political order: 'The Law shall still direct my peacefull Sway,/And the same Law teach Rebels to Obey'. The quasi-paradoxical qualities of the hero, his love of valour and peace, glory and public duty, have become generalized as mercy and power, and are now principles of government.

At the end of 'Annus Mirabilis' the virtues and powers of the hero do not lead the poet into the prophecy of happiness for England; rather, the military and mercantile forces give promise in that poem of the earthly paradise.

> Thus to the Eastern wealth through storms we go;
> But now, the Cape once doubled, fear no more:
> A constant Trade-wind will securely blow,
> And gently lay us on the Spicy shore.
> (lines 1213–16)

And while earlier the goodness of the king was proclaimed to be above the law, the 'Lawful Lord' restored at the end of 'Absalom and Achitophel' receives his power and position, not from an individual will directed towards the good of the state, but from the strength and established order of the nation itself. The notion that one man may exercise his will upon the state belongs to rebels who are driven from the kingdom. While one image must not be given too much importance, it is significant that the king in 'Absalom and Achitophel' says, 'Kings are the public Pillars of the State,/Born to sustain and prop the Nations weight', a new picture of the hero's function and one in strong contrast to the astronomical images that earlier defined his role.

That the importance of the king in 'Annus Mirabilis' is not self-evident and that the king's speech in 'Absalom and Achitophel' is a weak and unsatisfying conclusion to an otherwise heroic and vigorous poem point out the differences in the function of the hero in these two works from that in earlier ones. The king acts as a hero, but his figure lacks majesty. It is too convenient to say that the weakness of Charles II caused the transformation; the diminution of the hero could have been predicted from Dryden's ideas of society, its organic nature, its union of mutually dependent forces, epitomized but not controlled by the hero. Dryden's vision of the state destroyed the idealization of the representative of the state.

If Dryden's doubts about the value of the traditional hero seriously
weakened the conclusions of 'Annus Mirabilis' and 'Absalom and
Achitophel', they totally ruined the last two poems in which Dryden
has a ceremonial hero as the subject. 'Threnodia Augustalis' and
'Britannia Rediviva' are riddled with poetical clichés, inappropriate
similes, and bombast. Since Dryden was writing some of his best
poetry at this time and since he had written very good panegyrics earlier,
it is not far-fetched to suppose that the faults result to a great degree
from a distrust of the notions of heroism that, because of the position
of the two men, Dryden felt required to present. Intellectual misgivings
about a leader stronger than the nation would tolerate or dedicated to
goals not popular with the people are principal causes of the technical
flaws.

Although there are unfortunate references to Niobe, to the lack of a
'wrinkle' in the sky, and to 'an Hurricane on *Indian* Seas', the first
stanza of 'Threnodia Augustalis' has dignity, and tension is created by
the contrast of the general peace with the news, '*Our Gracious Prince
was dead*'. The simile of Atlas falling is apt and well-controlled until
the last line, 'Our *Atlas* fell indeed; But *Hercules* was near'. When
James is described in the second stanza, there is a change in the length
of the lines and in diction to suggest domestic piety, which clashes with
the allusion to Hercules. The ballad metre and the over-familiar diction
contrast too sharply with the tone of the first stanza, and when Dryden
attempts to raise the tone, he fails.

> Half unarray'd he ran to his Relief,
> So hasty and so artless was his grief:
> Approaching Greatness met him with her Charms
>   Of Pow'r and future State.   (lines 54–7)

'Half unarray'd' James could properly run to his brother's bedside, but
in dishabille the hero should not encounter a personified figure. When
Charles is seen, he is named, 'God's Image'; following this, he is termed,
'A Senseless Lump of sacred Clay', a distasteful image that is almost
blasphemous. In this poem Dryden employs characteristic techniques
that do not succeed. Starting with a historical framework, the poet
usually orders events and places them in a cultural perspective so that
their significance is understood. Here the subjects are too exactly
described; the allusions are tacked on, are not blended with history to
suggest a theme that might grow out of the action.

It can simply be stated that faults similar to those in 'Threnodia
Augustalis' reappear in 'Britannia Rediviva'. But the latter poem is
important for our purposes. The conclusion, restrained in its praise
and hesitating in its promise of happiness, demonstrates Dryden's new
attitude towards the national hero, and strongly contrasts with the
pictures of the future earthly paradise and the astronomical imagery
that characterized the prophecies of the early poems. The poet now

explicitly refuses the hero a destiny that would be separate from his role in society. 'Justice' is the one attribute that Dryden assigns James; the goodness that allows the king to be above the law is not hinted at.[4] Dryden warns James specifically against attempting to be a traditional hero.

> Some Kings the name of Conq'rours have assum'd,
> Some to be Great, some to be Gods presum'd;
> But boundless pow'r, and arbitrary Lust
> Made Tyrants still abhor the Name of Just.
>
> .   .   .   .
>
> But Justice is Heav'ns self, so strictly He,
> That cou'd it fail, the God-head cou'd not be.
> This Virtue is your own; but Life and State
> Are One to Fortune subject, One to Fate.
> (lines 339–42; 355–8)

Although Dryden was constantly aware in his early poems of the disruptive elements in the kingdom, he could praise the king or hero as a figure that would unite the conflicting forces while he also pictures him as a separate being with a unique destiny, joining the Renaissance ideal of heroism with the growing concern in the Restoration with the social order. When Dryden attempts to picture such a hero in his later poems, he fails chiefly because he does not believe that the hero should act except as a part of the social and political system. Even in 'Annus Mirabilis' and 'Absalom and Achitophel' the hero could be praised for performing his task. Now the occasions of the poems force the poet to extol the hero in the manner of the early panegyrics while Dryden is more interested in the social order and its preservation.

The ceremonial hero, then, is a principal figure in Dryden's poetry, and was the first important poetic device used by the poet to reflect his ideas about society and the hero's place in it. While the persons transformed into the hero, except for those in 'To Dr Charleton', are in political affairs, they need not be since the figure is representative of national goals and spiritual aspirations that are not limited to the political realm; the person certainly need not be the king. Such a hero is a perfect means for uniting historical material with the theme of regeneration and for announcing the glorious future possible for England. Yet since Dryden is concerned throughout his poetry more with the total structure of society than with its representative, it is no surprise that the hero plays a less important role in the later poems, and that when the notion of the hero seemed to conflict with the aims of the social order, the poet withdraws his sympathy from the hero. When Dryden employs the theme of redemption in his later poetry, he turns

---

[4] For a discussion of Dryden's personal misgivings about James II see Charles E. Ward, *The Life of John Dryden*, Chapel Hill, 1961, pp. 222–38.

to a figure more obviously associated with regeneration, a woman—
Anne Killigrew, St Cecilia, the Duchess of Ormond—abandoning the
ceremonial hero, which had already outlived its artistic usefulness.

From 'Dryden's Ceremonial Hero', *Studies in English Literature*,
Vol. 9, No. 3, 1969, pp. 379–93 (379–93).

The Essay *Of Dramatic Poesy*

We are accustomed to reading 'Of Dramatic Poesy' as a debate, a battle-ground of English versus French and Ancient versus Modern. If, however, the essay is considered as the ground for a struggle between literal and ideal representation, the lines can be drawn in quite a different way. Let us examine the work in this light. Eugenius and Neander accept Lisideius' definition, but Crites raises the 'logical objection' that it fails to differentiate drama from other literary forms (I, 25). Immediately a basic line of dispute is clear: Crites upholds and the others tend to belittle generic distinctions. In an earlier chapter I noted that in the definition Dryden was preparing for an explicit denial of them. Near the end of the last speech Neander says in comparing tragedy with epic:

> For though tragedy be justly preferred above the other, yet there is a great affinity between them, as may easily be discovered in that definition of a play which Lisideius gave us. The genus of them is the same, a just and lively image of human nature, in its actions, passions, and traverses of fortune: so is the end, namely for the delight and benefit of mankind. The characters and persons are still the same, viz. the greatest of both sorts; only the manner of acquainting us with those actions, passions, and fortunes, is different. Tragedy performs it *viva voce*, or by action, in dialogue; wherein it excels the epic poem, which does it chiefly by narration, and therefore is not so lively an image of human nature. (I, 87–8)

Dryden was to change his mind about the relative merits of the two forms, and during the 1670s he was forced to pay more attention to the generic demands of drama, but nonetheless his tendency to conflate the two forms is apparent even in the 1690s. We might guess then that in 'Of Dramatic Poesy' there will be a conflict between a point of view which emphasizes *representation* as the essence of drama and one which regards it as no more than a lively way of conveying the author's imitation to his audience. Crites takes the former view, Lisideius and Neander the latter, and Eugenius tends to agree with them.

The issue is simple: what constitutes the imitation of nature? Crites' two speeches (the first and fifth of the six) contain demands for observance of the three unities and the avoidance of rime; he is for the 'nearest' imitation. His arguments are straightforward. First, the illusion of watching an action will be more difficult to maintain if great

amounts of time are supposed to elapse. Second, the scene must stay
close to the same place,

> for the stage on which it is represented being but one and the same
> place, it is unnatural to conceive it many, and those far distant from
> one another. I will not deny but, by the variation of painted scenes,
> the fancy (which in these cases will contribute to its own deceit) may
> sometimes imagine it several places, with some appearance of prob-
> ability; yet it still carries the greater likelihood of truth if those places
> be supposed so near each other, as in the same town or city; which
> may all be comprehended under the larger denomination of one
> place. (I, 29)

Third, one main action is all that can reasonably be followed at once.
Lastly, the condemnation of rime is based on explicitly naturalistic
premises.

> I am of opinion that rhyme is unnatural in a play, because dialogue
> there is presented as the effect of sudden thought. For a play is the
> imitation of nature; and since no man without premeditation speaks
> in rhyme, neither ought he to do it on the stage. . . . Nor will it serve
> you to object that . . . 'tis still known to be a play; and, consequently,
> the dialogue of two persons understood to be the labour of one poet.
> For a play is still an imitation of nature; we know we are to be
> deceived, and we desire to be so; but no man ever was deceived but
> with a probability of truth, for who will suffer a gross lie to be fastened
> on him? Thus we sufficiently understand that the scenes which
> represent cities and countries to us are not really such, but only
> painted on boards and canvas: but shall that excuse the ill painture or
> designment of them? Nay, rather ought they not to be laboured with
> so much the more diligence and exactness, to help the imagination?
> since the mind of man does naturally tend to, and seek after truth;
> and therefore the nearer any thing comes to the imitation of it, the
> more it pleases. (I, 78–80)

This position is essentially that stated by Howard in the Preface to *The
Duke of Lerma*; here, as in Dryden's reply to that work in his 'Defence
of "An Essay" ', the conflict is between literal and nonliteral theories de
imitation. The identification of Crites with Howard's position is maan
essentially explicit when Dryden rather unfairly brings Crites to of
early conclusion with the statement that his arguments against rime 'are
for the most part already public' (I, 81).[1] It is sometimes objected against
the identification of Crites with Howard that Dryden could not properly
have made him the champion of the Ancients, since Howard had
publicly written that he could 'presume to say somthing in the justifica-

---

[1] The reference is evidently to Howard's Preface to *Four New Plays* (1665),
on which Dryden plainly drew in outlining Crites' position (see Spingarn,
Vol. 2, pp. 97–104.

tion of our Nations Plays', which, he claimed, 'justly challenge the Preheminence'.[2] In this respect, violence is done to Howard's position, but the bulk of what Crites is made to say has less to do with the relative merits of Ancients and Moderns than with the problems of how representation can be made effective.

If we try for the moment to forget the official lines of debate in 'Of Dramatic Poesy', we can see more clearly the basic conflict in the work. The first and third debates, generally regarded as Ancients versus Moderns and blank verse against rime, are actually about different parts of the same subject—whether Crites' demands for near-literal representation are justified. The middle debate, ostensibly French versus English, is postulated on Lisideius' assumption that imitation should *not* be literal; the actual disagreement there is largely on the question of how much literal restriction need remain. The essential denial of Crites' claims is made by Neander near the end of the essay:

> It has been formerly urged by you, and confessed by me, that since no man spoke any kind of verse *ex tempore*, that which was nearest nature was to be preferred. I answer you, therefore, by distinguishing betwixt what is nearest to the nature of comedy, which is the imitation of common persons and ordinary speaking, and *what is nearest the nature of a serious play*: this last is indeed the representation of nature, but 'tis *nature wrought up to an higher pitch*. The plot, the characters, the wit, the passions, the descriptions, are all *exalted above the level of common converse*, as high as the imagination of the poet can carry them with proportion to verisimility. Tragedy, we know, is wont to image to us the minds and fortunes of noble persons, and to portray these exactly; heroic rhyme is nearest nature, as being the noblest kind of modern verse. (I, 86–7; italics added)

If we study the structure of the essay in light of this dispute, it looks something like this.

(1) Crites demands literal representation on the ground that it is most pleasing. Eugenius speaks against the unity of place as an excessive modern restriction (I, 36), but his basic counterclaim is that a serious writer should 'stir up a pleasing admiration and concernment, which are the objects of a tragedy' (I, 41). Crites' concern is for the representation, Eugenius' for the effect. In place of an imitation whose exactness is to be admired, Eugenius praises art which affects the spectator, often through display of love and tenderness (I, 41–2). These affective assumptions underlie the second exchange, whose subject (from this perspective) is how the effect is best obtained.

(2) Lisideius praises the unities (of which the French had made a great deal), but, significantly, he devotes most of his attention to unity of action—which Crites had mentioned only briefly and indifferently (cf. I, 29–30). Lisideius follows 'Aristotle' in saying that the 'end of

[2] Preface to *Four New Plays*, Spingarn, Vol. 2, pp. 98, 100.

tragedies *or serious plays* . . . is to beget *admiration*, compassion, or concernment' (I, 46; italics added).[3] The emphasis on unity of action may seem momentarily surprising. After all, Lisideius' definition omits all mention of action. But his point is that in order to get maximum effect, the dramatist must concentrate on a single, unified incident, refining away all extraneous events and characters in the process.[4] Lisideius does say flatly that 'the spirit of man cannot be satisfied but with truth, or at least verisimility' (I, 47)—hence his suggestion that a play be 'grounded upon some known history' (I, 46). The object, however, is to *suggest* verisimilitude, not to dramatize history, for the author's job is to interweave truth with 'probable fiction' in order to mend the 'intrigues of fate' and dispense a pleasing poetic justice (I, 47). Like Eugenius and Neander, Lisideius feels that a story whose end is known to the audience will rouse less concern than one which keeps it in suspense. But the key to Lisideius' whole view of drama lies in his reservations about the effectiveness of representation.

> I have observed that, in all our tragedies, the audience cannot forbear laughing when the actors are to die; 'tis the most comic part of the whole play. All *passions* may be lively represented on the stage . . . but there are many *actions* which can never be imitated to a just height: dying especially is a thing which none but a Roman gladiator could naturally perform on the stage, when he did not imitate or represent, but naturally do it; and therefore it is better to omit the representation of it.
>
> The words of a good writer, which describe it lively, will make a deeper impression of belief in us than all the actor can persuade us to when he seems to fall dead before us; as a poet in the description of a beautiful garden, or a meadow, will please our imagination more than the place itself can please our sight. When we see death represented, we are convinced it is but fiction; but when we hear it related, our eyes (the strongest witnesses) are wanting, which might have undeceived us, and we are all willing to favour the sleight when the poet does not too grossly impose on us. . . . But it is objected that if one part of the play may be related, then why not all? I answer, some parts of the action are more fit to be represented, some to be related. (I, 51–2)

Thus he places the verbal and poetic part of drama far above the visual. Representation, the prime differential between drama and other literary forms, becomes here merely a minor adjunct.

Neander starts his reply by saying that he will 'grant Lisideius,

[3] 'Admiration' was a sixteenth-century addition. But in it and in the mention of the 'serious play' we can see in capsule the theory of the Restoration heroic play.

[4] For a helpful discussion of the nature of the French drama which serves Lisideius as a model, see Elder Olson, *Tragedy and the Theory of Drama*, Detroit, 1961, Chapter 9.

without much dispute, a great part of what he has urged against us' (referring to his strictures on the Elizabethans). Many of his objections are against Lisideius' concessions to representational verisimilitude. Thus Neander quotes Corneille on the excessive restrictions on invention (and even probability) imposed by the unities, and he is readier to accept dramatic illusion:

> The indecency of tumults is all which can be objected against fighting: for why may not our imagination as well suffer itself to be deluded with the probability of it, as with any other thing in the play? For my part, I can with as great ease persuade myself that the blows which are struck are given in good earnest, as I can that they who strike them are Kings or princes, or those persons which they represent. (I, 62)[5]

Neander's principal claim for the English, however, is that their imitation of nature is *lively* and therefore better fitted to 'beget concernment in us' (I, 60) than the relatively 'cold' French manner. But Neander agrees with Lisideius on the object of serious drama (to rouse admiration, compassion, and concernment in the audience) and in the proper subject for imitation: 'The soul of poesy . . . is imitation of humour and passions' (I, 56).

(3) In the final debate Crites challenges Lisideius and Neander on the use of rime, holding that it renders the author's imitation of nature unnatural. This discussion is often skimmed over, for in and of itself rime is not an issue which enthralls us. Actually, half hidden in this wrangle over the suitability and utility of rime in plays is the more basic issue of literal versus heightened representation. I have already quoted Crites' objections and Neander's reply that rime helps 'exalt' a serious play 'above the level of common converse'. The details are not important. What matters is Neander's conclusion: 'A play, as I have said, to be like nature, is to be set above it' (I, 88).[6]

[5] Neander seems to be stretching a point here. In a real debate a believer in literal representation would undoubtedly have objected. After all, the spectator is not asked to *believe* any of these pretences, but merely to suffer the illusion. All men look alike, whether prince or actor, but very seldom does a feigned blow *appear* real. Neander's point on fighting seems to be a pragmatic allowance on Dryden's part, for as Neander is made to say just before this, 'custom has so insinuated itself into our countrymen . . . [that] they will scarcely suffer combats and other objects of horror to be taken from them' (I, 62).

[6] Although I owe Dean T. Mace ('Dryden's Dialogue on Drama', *Journal of the Warburg and Courtauld Institute*, Vol. 25, 1962, pp. 87–112) an obvious debt for suggesting this general line of approach to 'Of Dramatic Poesy', I am not altogether in agreement with many of his specific interpretations. Basically, I feel that he overemphasizes the connection of Neander's principle of 'variety' to literal representation (p. 107); that in general he does not realize how much of Lisideius' position is actually absorbed into Neander's; and that he exaggerates in saying that Lisideius 'offers a dramatic structure unlimited by the necessity of conforming to anything but an inward and hidden psychological truth' (p. 110)— this ignores the import of Lisideius' genuine concern for the unities.

We have all become accustomed to the idea that one of the main objects in 'Of Dramatic Poesy' was to put down the French, but whatever Dryden's opinion of the relative merits of contemporary French and English drama, French ideas are both stronger and more pervasive in the essay than has generally been supposed. In both the definition and in Neander's speeches Dryden follows the French stress on passions at the expense of action. In the 'Defence of "An Essay" ' Dryden is pushed into admitting more explicitly the anti-naturalistic nature of his views; grudgingly he admits that he calls rime 'natural' not because it is 'nearest the nature of that it represents' (which it obviously is not), but because he considers it most fitted to the nature of 'a serious subject' (I, 113). And on the issue of dramatic illusion he is driven to grant that he is relying on 'the imagination of the audience, aided by the words of the poet, and painted scenes' to compensate for infractions against the unities (I, 125).

The true import of the 'Essay' and its 'Defence', if I understand them rightly, is essentially that Dryden was pulling away from a literal concept of the representation of nature in drama and moving toward a more imaginative and anti-realistic one. Not only was a selection to be made to increase the impact of what was 'imitated', but the elements selected were to be worked up, 'wrought up to an higher pitch' in order to affect the audience more strongly. And since, obviously, this could not be done visually, the visual aspect of drama is downgraded in favour of the verbal.

From Chapter 6 of *Dryden's Criticism*, Ithaca, New York, 1970, pp. 187–230 (195–203).

The Personal Drama of Dryden's
The Hind and the Panther

'The Hind and the Panther', though recognized as a major poem by a major poet, remains unappreciated by the general public, being read chiefly for some brilliant passages rather than as a whole. An opinion about the poem expressed some thirty-five years ago in the *Times Literary Supplement* will still seem valid to many: 'The poem, partly owing to the subject and partly to its references of ephemeral interest . . . has long been a somewhat faded masterpiece, often praised for its style and almost as often condemned for its substance'.[1] A recent general introduction to Dryden dismisses the poem as 'versified theology': ' "The Hind and the Panther" . . . consists mainly of a disputation between a "milk white Hind, immortal and unchanged" (the Catholic Church) and a female Panther (the Church of England) about the history of schism, papal infallibility and transubstantiation, etc.'[2] Many readers would probably support Dr Samuel Johnson's lukewarm praise of the poem as 'an example of poetical ratiocination' distinguished by its prosodic skill.[3] Recently, F. T. Prince has assigned the work a central place in the understanding of Dryden; but his brief appreciation, which emphasizes 'the extraordinary mastery' of style, does little more than suggest that the poem is valuable in demonstrating Dryden's great versatility as a stylist.[4] The general impression of the poem remains unchallenged: its subject is theological, it is ratiocinative or argumentative in method, and it is distinguished in its poetic style. There has been no real recognition of a basic fact about the poem: that it is an intensely personal confession of faith, and that the personal drama of faith makes the poem a moving and vital literary work, rich in content, complex in method, and more unified in structure than is generally recognized. . . . This general estimate needs to be re-evaluated; for it seems a serious critical oversight to pay so little attention to the personal drama of Dryden, which is not only a major element in the poem but its most appealing and universal subject.

[1] 'Dryden's Conversion: The Struggle for Faith', *TLS*, 17 April 1937, p. 281.
[2] Dennis Davison, *Dryden*, London, 1968, p. 141. For stress on the ideas in the poem, see Victor M. Hamm, 'Dryden's "The Hind and the Panther" and Roman Catholic Apologetics', *PMLA*, 83, May, 1968, pp. 400–15.
[3] Samuel Johnson, 'Dryden', *Lives of the English Poets*, ed. George Birkbeck Hill, Oxford, 1905, Vol. 1, p. 446.
[4] F. T. Prince, 'Dryden Redivivus', *REL*, 1, 1960, pp. 71–9.

In a recent literary history, it has been suggested that the poem is indeed personal: 'We read the poem because it is a pleasure to be with Dryden; it is the mind of Dryden that we are in contact with, and the voice of Dryden that we hear throughout. This alone gives the poem any unity it may have.'[5] The insight is sound, but the modern rhetorical interest in 'the voice' adds little to the earlier scholarly interest in 'the mind of Dryden'.[6] Critics today shy away from the biographical approach to a literary work, and hence miss the intensely felt personal confession of Dryden's spiritual struggle. The writer in the *Times Literary Supplement*, in a period when the biographical approach was more respectable, in fact lamented: 'It is a thousand pities that Dryden did not conceive the poem as a simple and straightforward *confessio fidei*, instead of attempting a "beast-fable", of which he was not a master. . . .'[7] But 'The Hind and the Panther' is precisely that—a confession of faith—though hardly 'simple and straightforward'. And the effective literary treatment of this confession, far more complex and personal than that in 'Religio Laici', is made possible by the beast fable. A primary fact that needs to be recognized is that both the Panther and the Hind are personae representing Dryden; and a major element in the poem is the dramatic revelation of the poet's mind and spirit in crisis.

In the poem, Dryden lays bare his religious struggle, both intellectual and spiritual—the one resolved but dramatized as a debate in the present, the other still in progress and unresolved. It is this personal revelation that makes the poem moving, human, and appealing. It is not autobiography in the usual sense; and as Harth suggests, 'When approached from the viewpoint of biography, it is a baffling document'.[8] Dryden is not presenting data about himself in the ordinary sense; it is not his 'Grace Abounding to the Chief of Sinners', setting forth the long agonizing struggle to achieve faith. It is rather the personal revelation of a neoclassical poet, and hence an artful treatment of autobiography. The confession is transformed in two characteristically neoclassical ways: 1. the theme, the *confessio fidei*, is universalized through treating the poet's experience as a pattern of the universal Christian experience; 2. the confession is dramatized, and hence objectified, through the literary strategy of the beast fable. These two objectives, the universalization of the autobiographical material and the literary treatment, may obscure for the modern reader the deeply personal drama enacted in the poem. Above all, the role of the Panther, who is sometimes the persona of the poet, needs to be recognized; for it is through the skilful handling of both the Hind and the Panther that

[5] James Sutherland, *English Literature of the Late Seventeenth Century*, New York, 1969, p. 191.

[6] For the study of Dryden's mind, see Louis I. Bredvold, *The Intellectual Milieu of John Dryden*, Ann Arbor, 1934.

[7] *TLS*, p. 281.

[8] Phillip Harth, *Contexts of Dryden's Thought*, Chicago, 1968, p. 244.

Dryden effectively transforms the poem into something more than an argumentative piece about points of dogma.

The precise nature of the personal element also needs clarification, since there is some confusion about the matter. Earl Miner expresses the generally accepted view when he remarks that each of the three parts has 'a personal or confessional passage of uncommon interest'.[9] In particular, lines 72–8 in Part I, beginning, 'My thoughtless youth was wing'd with vain desires', and lines 277–305 in Part III, have been recognized as striking instances of this fact. In the preface 'To the Reader', Dryden himself calls attention to the autobiographical element: 'What I desire the *Reader* should know concerning me, he will find in the Body of the Poem; if he have but the patience to peruse it.'[10] To this he adds: ' 'Tis evident that some part of it was only occasional, & not first intended. I mean that defence of my self, to which every honest man is bound, when he is injuriously attacqu'd in Print. . . .'[11] The second passage is taken to refer to lines 218–60 in Part III in which the poet defends himself against the attacks of Anglican foes like Edward Stillingfleet. The accepted critical view is that the autobiographical element appears in *specific* and *explicit* passages, either of confession or self-defence. It is not recognized, however, that the personal element appears more importantly throughout the poem, often *implicitly*, in the encounters between the Hind and the Panther. As Dryden says, the reader will find this 'in the Body of the Poem; if he have but the patience to peruse it'.

In the current shying away from the biographical approach to a literary work, the critic is likely to miss Dryden's hint. In fact, even the 'occasional' personal passages have been dismissed in a recent study as part of Dryden's rhetorical strategy. Of Dryden's statements in the preface, Harth remarks: 'He is referring, not to information about himself, in the usual sense, but to two passages in the poem which draw attention to himself in order to establish subjective *ethos*.'[12] According to this view, the explicitly personal passages are to be regarded primarily as part of a rhetorical strategy to win the sympathy of the reader. The lines in Part I beginning, 'My thoughtless youth was wing'd with vain desires' have been accepted as an explicit description of Dryden's spiritual and intellectual career up to his conversion ever since Sir Walter Scott singled them out for special comment in his life of Dryden.[13] But according to Harth, 'the purpose of this passage is not

---

[9] Earl Miner, *Dryden's Poetry*, Bloomington, 1967, p. 146. Miner characterizes the personal passages as 'the most interesting unifying device' in the poem, in *The Works of John Dryden, Vol. III : Poems 1685–1692*, ed. Earl Miner, Berkeley, 1969, p. 346.

[10] Miner, *Works of Dryden*, Vol. 3, p. 119. All quotations from the poem and its preface are from this text.

[11] Ibid., p. 121.

[12] Harth, p. 51.

[13] Sir Walter Scott, *The Life of John Dryden*, ed. Bernard Kreissman, Lincoln, Nebr., 1963, p. 262.

autobiographical, but rhetorical': 'Dryden enhances the impression of sincerity and humility' through the confession and thus achieves the primary purpose of disarming the unsympathetic reader.[14] Although one may accept the possibility of a rhetorical strategy in any poetic statement, this kind of critical approach minimizes the intensely realized personal drama which gives the poem its vitality.

The passage in question is in fact intimately autobiographical, and its primary literary function is to provide a key to the personal meaning of the poem. It not only recapitulates the *past* history of Dryden's religious experience, as most critics have assumed; but it is also an explicit statement of the spiritual struggle in the *present*. An examination of the passage indeed supports such an interpretation.

> My thoughtless youth was wing'd with vain desires,
> My manhood, long misled by wandring fires,
> Follow'd false lights; and when their glimps was gone,
> My pride struck out new sparkles of her own.
> Such was I, such by nature still I am,
> Be thine the glory, and be mine the shame.
> Good life be now my task: my doubts are done.
>   (I, 72–8)

The lines refer to two kinds of struggle, one intellectual and the other spiritual. The intellectual struggle, involving dogmatic issues and chiefly the question of church authority, has been resolved; for Dryden concludes line 78 with the statement, 'my doubts are done'. If this resolution of his intellectual doubts was achieved, it was due to God's grace in opening his eyes.[15] In the poem, this intellectual struggle is dramatized as a debate in the present time between Hind and Panther, chiefly in Part II.[16] But the spiritual struggle remains unresolved: the 'false lights' and 'wandring fires' of Dryden's past (his Anglican views and possibly his dallying with deism) sprang from his 'pride', and this pride is innate. This inborn pride of the poet, though recognized as the source of past errors, remains a basic part of his nature; it is still a source of conflict and shame, since the true Christian spirit demands humility. 'Good life be now my task', says the poet. The dramatic presentation of the poet's

[14] Harth, p. 52. In fairness to Harth, one should note his qualification: 'To point out the rhetorical effectiveness in the poem of such reminders is not to question the sincerity of Dryden's declaration or the genuineness of his feelings. It is simply to recognize that these passages serve a deliberate rhetorical function as a mode of persuasion carefully subordinated to Dryden's general purpose in the poem and to his awareness of his audience' (p. 54).

[15] See letter to Mrs Steward, 7 November 1699: 'May God be pleasd to open your Eyes, as he has opend mine'—*The Letters of John Dryden*, ed. Charles E. Ward, Durham, 1942, p. 124.

[16] This idea has been suggested by Earl Miner, in 'The Significance of Plot in "The Hind and the Panther" ', *BNYPL*, 69, 1965, p. 454: 'One possibility is . . . that the debate between the Hind and the Panther mirrors a debate in Dryden's own mind from about that date' (July, 1685, possibly the date of his conversion).

not wholly successful effort to humble his pride, an effort that must be sustained in the present and the future, is a major element in the poem; and in the literary handling of this theme, the Panther often represents the poet in his worldly pride both past and present.

It might be argued against this view that the Panther has always been regarded as representing the Church of England. But in so far as the poem dramatically recapitulates in debate the dogmatic position abandoned by Dryden, a position set forth clearly in 'Religio Laici', it can be said that the Panther stands not only for the Anglican Church but for Dryden's former views. Further, the Panther is the embodiment of the pride that led to Dryden's following false lights. In contrast to Catholic humility, symbolized by the Hind's 'Contempt of wealth, and willfull poverty' (II, 715), the Panther represents worldliness, whether of Anglicans or the former Anglican poet.[17] The worldly pride of the Panther is opposed to the Hind's humility and charity; but in so far as the poet confesses to the pride that dwells in his heart still, the Panther is an embodiment of that unvanquished pride.

Of course, the Panther and the Hind are far more than representations of Dryden, since, as Earl Miner points out, the 'poem employs a discontinuous fable or intermittent allegory . . .';[18] and the two beasts represent a variety of people, positions, and postures. As Miner further suggests, 'Dryden's . . . animals . . . may be looked upon as types whose attributes develop in time and history, while their essences remain the same'.[19] By using traditional beast lore, Dryden is able to embody a complex of established meanings in beasts that are typological and symbolic.[20] Essentially, the Hind and the Panther represent the basic polarity between the Christian spirit and the non-Christian spirit—of humility and charity (Hind) versus pride and malice (Panther).[21] They also embody, in a descending degree of particularity in historical time, these other polarities: the Catholic (true) Church, characterized by the true Christian spirit versus the Anglican (false) Church, characterized by pride and worldliness. Also Catholics versus Anglicans, distinguished by a difference in dogmatic certitude and Christian spirit. Thus Stillingfleet is a more particular instance of the Panther, and Dryden a more particular instance of the Hind (and hence, too, the poet is a pattern of the Catholic and true Christian).

---

[17] Though the discovery of precise allegories can become a pedantic exercise, one might note that the Panther's lechery (I, 351–75), fashionable quality (I, 572), and witty raillery (II, 60–9) echo qualities we associate with Dryden when he was an Anglican: his licentious comedies, which he regretted in his Catholic period, and his pride in his success as a wit at Court in the early 1670s.

[18] Miner, *Works of Dryden*, Vol. 3, p. 341.

[19] Miner, *Dryden's Poetry*, p. 163.

[20] James Kinsley, 'Dryden's Bestiary', *RES*, n.s. 4, 1953, p. 332; also Miner, *Dryden's Poetry*, Chapter 5.

[21] The Panther and the Hind are distinguished by 'two essentially different moral natures'—George Wasserman, 'Note on Dryden's Panther', *N&Q*, 13, October, 1966, p. 382.

Beyond this, in so far as the two beasts represent two polar qualities (the true Christian, marked by charity and humility, versus the false Christian, marked by pride and malice), the Hind and the Panther symbolize the conflicting tendencies in Dryden himself. On the intellectual level, the conflict between the true and the false is resolved through debate over the question of authority. On the spiritual level, the conflict between humility and pride is never wholly resolved, and thus provides the moving spectacle of the continuing struggle by the poet to achieve the true Christian spirit. The great advantage of the beast fable is that through it Dryden is able to present his own personal spiritual and intellectual struggle, and at the same time raise it to the level of a more general statement, both temporal-historical (the Catholic-Anglican conflict in the reign of James II) and universal (the Christian-worldly conflict, which is the essence of the Christian's struggle toward a good life). We need now to examine more closely the working out of this complex literary treatment. Since the intellectual struggle involving the debate over authority has received considerable attention, though in purely impersonal terms, we should turn to the poet's struggle to suppress his pride. Ultimately, this intimate personal struggle is the most vital religious and literary element in the poem, the one element in fact which is likely to arouse a keen interest in the general reader.

Dryden's assumption of a sympathetic persona in the Hind is understandable as a rhetorical strategy. But it also represents Dryden's sincere effort to assume the character of a humble, forgiving Christian in contrast to the proud, malicious Panther. Yet the character of the Hind was at odds with the poet's fundamentally aggressive and even vindictive nature (at least by his own confession); and this gives rise in the poem to an intense struggle between his innate pride and his Christian ideal. That pride and the desire for revenge, represented by the Panther, were very much a part of Dryden's nature after his conversion is evident from other sources. In 1693, in the 'Discourse Concerning the Original and Progress of Satire', Dryden justified lampoons or personal attacks on several grounds:

The first is Revenge, when we have been affronted in the same Nature, or have been any ways notoriously abus'd, and can make our selves no other Reparation. And yet we know, that, in Christian Charity, all Offences are to be forgiven; as we expect the like Pardon for those which we daily commit against Almighty God. And this Consideration has often made me tremble when I was saying our Saviour's Prayer; for the plain Condition of the forgiveness which we beg, is the pardoning of others the Offences which they have done to us: For which Reason I have many times avoided the Commission of that Fault; ev'n when I have been notoriously provok'd. . . . I have seldom answer'd any scurrilous Lampoon: When it was in my power to have expos'd my Enemies: And being naturally vindicative, have suffer'd in silence; and possess'd my Soul in quiet.[22]

Yet revenge lurked as a strong motive in the poet's heart; and the advantage of the beast fable is that Dryden was able to assimilate it into the dramatic presentation of the struggle in himself between charity and revenge.

The beast fable actually permitted Dryden to achieve two contradictory goals: to dramatize his own spiritual struggle, in which the Hind becomes the symbol of his success, and at the same time to defend himself against Anglican charges and also counter-attack. The defence of himself against charges of venality was a difficult one; but it is made plausible through the use of the Hind, which permits the poet to adopt the posture of the injured, innocent Christian. The counter-attack then becomes an expression of righteous anger by the Hind. The complexity of the strategies and the intensely personal dilemma of the vengeful poet committed to charity are suggested by the contrast between 'The Hind and the Panther' and an earlier polemical work in which Dryden directly attacked his Anglican enemy.

This polemical piece was part of a public controversy in which Dryden became involved with Edward Stillingfleet shortly after he became a Catholic. Their debate was acrimonious in the fashion of Restoration polemics, and it shows that Dryden could be malicious and un-Christian despite his conversion. The immediate occasion for the quarrel was the publication by James II of two papers found in his brother's strong box, giving reasons to prove that the Catholic Church was the only true church, and a third paper by Anne Hyde, first Duchess of York, giving the reasons for her conversion in 1670. Stillingfleet stood forth as the champion of the Anglican Church by publicly refuting these papers in print. This called forth a Catholic rebuttal, with three parts corresponding to the three divisions of Stillingfleet's refutation. The last of the three Catholic pieces was by Dryden, in defence of the Duchess's paper. This was actually part of a larger religious controversy that raged at this time over such matters as church authority and transubstantiation. Dryden's purely polemical work is direct in its attack, conventional in its arguments, and at times vituperative. Its relationship to 'The Hind and the Panther' is much like that of Dryden's Tory pamphlet of 1681, 'His Majesties Declaration Defended' to 'Absalom and Achitophel'. In both instances, the polemical work is direct, prosaic, and argumentative, and presents the official position of the Court or Church. In contrast, the poems not only metamorphose the arguments, presenting Dryden's personal views, but also transcend the topical limitations and become complex poetic statements with universal meanings.

In the quarrel with Stillingfleet, the talented Catholic convert was the

[22] *The Poems of John Dryden*, ed. James Kinsley, Oxford, 1958, Vol. 2, p. 646.

aggressor in the attack on the learned divine; and Dryden's polemical tone suggests the tone of the Panther in its harshness. In his opening remarks, Dryden paints a picture of the Duchess much like that of the Hind, and in contrast, he ascribes to Stillingfleet qualities later assigned the Panther:

> I Dare appeal to all unprejudic'd Readers, and especially to those who have any sense of Piety, whether upon Perusal of the Paper written by Her late Highness the Duchess, they have not found in it somewhat which touch'd them to the very Soul; whether they did not plainly and perfectly discern in it the Spirit of Meekness, Devotion, and Sincerity, which animates the whole Discourse. . . . And now let any unbiass'd and indifferent Reader compare the Spirit of the Answerer with hers. Do's there not manifestly appear in him a quite different Character? Need the Reader be inform'd, that he is disingenuous, foul-mouth'd, and shuffling; and that, not being able to answer plain Matter of Fact, he endeavours to evade it, by Suppositions, Circumstances, and Conjectures; like a cunning Barreter of Law, who is to manage a sinking Cause, the Dishonesty of which he cannot otherwise support, than by defaming his Adversary.[23]

Dryden's sharp rebuttal brought an acrimonious reply from Stillingfleet. In his 'Vindication of the Answer to Some Late Papers', the Anglican divine called the reader's attention to Dryden's 'civil and obliging' description of him as '*disingenuous, foul-mouth'd*, and *shuffling*'. 'Is this indeed', he asked sarcastically, 'the Spirit of a *New Convert*? Is this the Meekness and Temper you intend to gain Proselites by, and to convert the Nation? . . . But Zeal in a new Convert is a terrible thing; for it not only burns, but rages, like the Eruptions of Mount *AEtna*. . . .'[24] In another passage, Stillingfleet questioned Dryden's competence in dogmatics for speaking of the Duchess's right to the use of her own judgement: 'But this Gentleman talks like a meer Novice as to Matters of Faith, as tho *believing* were *a new thing* to him. . . .'[25] Further, Stillingfleet made two charges that angered Dryden: first, that the poet was a 'nimble' convert because he really had no religion,[26] and second, that the poet had succumbed to the 'Temptation of changing his Religion for Bread'.[27] To such charges, Dryden responded with anger. But instead

---

[23] 'A Defence of the Papers', pp. 85–6. This accusation is not really fair to Stillingfleet, despite the mild sarcasm of the latter's 'Answer'. Dryden's historical arguments against Stillingfleet on the Reformation are superior to his theological.

[24] Edward Stillingfleet, *A Vindication of the Answer to Some Late Papers Concerning the Unity and Authority of the Catholick Church, and the Reformation of the Church of England*, London, 1687, p. 54.

[25] Ibid., p. 102.

[26] Ibid., p. 2.

[27] Ibid., p. 105.

of counter-attacking with the bludgeon of prose, he wisely exchanged that crude weapon for the sharp rapier of heroic couplets in his beast fable.

In 'The Hind and the Panther', Dryden's pride, anger, and vindictiveness are assimilated into the pattern of the poem, and become an essential element in the personal drama. Before defending himself against Stillingfleet's charges in Part III, Dryden provides a fuller characterization of the two beasts, since they are crucial to his self-defence and counter-attack. The Panther is more incisively sketched:

> Disdain, with gnawing envy, fell despight,
> And canker'd malice stood in open sight;
> Ambition, int'rest, pride without controul,
> And jealousie, the jaundice of the soul;
> Revenge, the bloudy minister of ill,
> With all the lean tormentors of the will.   (III, 70–5)

In contrast, the Hind is pictured as a patient and meek creature,

> whose noble nature strove
> T' express her plain simplicity of love.   (III, 30–1)

This clear characterization, with stress on malice and charity as key traits in the two beasts, is crucial for what follows, since the Hind's satirical remarks can now be interpreted as righteous indignation while those of the Panther can be attributed to malice. In the ensuing debate, the Hind is Dryden and the Panther is Stillingfleet, recapitulating the charges and countercharges of the polemical exchange earlier. By using these two personae, the poet gains an advantage over his adversary; for beyond establishing the proper character for each of the two antagonists, he creates an air of objectivity and fairness.

In the sharp exchange between the Hind and the Panther, it is actually the Hind who attacks first, assuming the tone of the satirist:

> Your sons of Latitude that court your grace,
> Though most resembling you in form and face,
> Are far the worst of your pretended race.
> And, but I blush your honesty to blot,
> Pray god you prove 'em lawfully begot:
> For, in some *Popish* libells I have read,
> The *Wolf* has been too busie in your bed.   (160–6)

The Hind insinuates that divines like Stillingfleet, besides being illegitimate in their doctrines, are also mercenary:

> Your sons of breadth at home, are much like these,
> Their soft and yielding metals run with ease,

> They melt, and take the figure of the mould:
> But harden, and preserve it best in gold.
>
> (III, 187–90)

To these insinuations, the Panther, already characterized as envious and malicious, responds by reciting Stillingfleet's charges against Dryden in his 'Vindication':

> Some sons of mine who bear upon their shield,
> Three steeples Argent in a sable field,
> Have sharply tax'd your converts, who unfed
> Have follow'd you for miracles of bread;
> Such who themselves of no religion are,
> Allur'd with gain, for any will declare.
>
> (193–8)

To these charges, which are seen as malicious in the dramatic context, the Hind offers a mild defence in keeping with her humility:

> Now for my converts, who you say unfed
> Have follow'd me for miracles of bread,
> Judge not by hear-say, but observe at least,
> If since their change, their loaves have been increast.
>
> (III, 221–4)

The advantage of Dryden's strategy in having the Hind defend him is that the modesty of the protest and its seeming objectivity are more persuasive than any defence by the poet *in propria persona*. The Hind adds:

> Mean-time my sons accus'd, by fames report
> Pay small attendance at the *Lyon*'s court.
> Nor rise with early crowds, nor flatter late,
> (For silently they beg who daily wait.)
>
> (III, 235–8)

In this agon, the Hind is allowed to feel righteous anger, at the same time maintaining the proper character of the meek and patient Christian:

> This said, she paus'd a little, and suppress'd
> The boiling indignation of her breast;
>
> (III, 261–2)

Leaving vengeance to God, she rebukes her son (Dryden), who is inclined to revenge—a strategy that adds to our sense of the Hind's fairness and objectivity by dissociating the Hind from Dryden. Having achieved this psychological advantage, the poet then has the Hind sharply rebuke the Panther's child (Stillingfleet):

It now remains for you to school your child,
And ask why *God*'s anointed he revil'd;
A *King* and *Princess* dead! did *Shimei* worse?
The curser's punishment should fright the curse:

(III, 306–9)

Though the Hind's remarks are sharp, we regard them as righteously motivated and justified. When she pauses momentarily, we learn that 'Glad was the *Panther* that the charge was clos'd' (line 341). This dramatization of the controversy with Stillingfleet through the animal fable not only gives Dryden the advantage, but it is a more exciting exchange than the earlier war of pamphlets. Through the contrasting personae of the Hind and the Panther, the poet can control his own complex involvement in the agon, as he variously becomes the Hind, one of the 'sons' of the Hind, and the narrator. He manages to defend himself against the charges of venality; he communicates the sense of his own humility; and at the same time he has his revenge.[28]

In the same manner, in the episode of the Buzzard, Dryden manages to gain revenge while maintaining his posture of humility. The Buzzard, in the ironic characterization, represents Gilbert Burnet, an Anglican clergyman toward whom Dryden felt considerable animus.[29] By putting the satirical strictures in the Hind's mouth, the poet escapes the charge of personal libel. Burnet was fair prey for any Catholic, since he was actively engaged in propaganda against James from his exile in Holland;[30] but Dryden may have had more personal reasons for his animosity, for there is Burnet's unverified story that the latter's criticism of Antoine Varillas's *Histoire des Revolutions arrivées dans l'Europe en Matière de Religion* kept Dryden from publishing a translation of the work. The sharp, yet witty attack on Burnet by the Hind is characteristic of Dryden in tone, method, and language:

A Theologue more by need, than genial bent,
By Breeding sharp, by Nature confident.
Int'rest in all his Actions was discern'd;
More learn'd than Honest, more a Wit than learn'd.
Or forc'd by Fear, or by his Profit led,
Or both conjoyn'd, his Native clyme he fled;

---

[28] Cf. III, 343–52, where Dryden justifies revenge:

For laws of arms permit each injur'd man,
To make himself a saver where he can. (343–4)

But Christianity requires forgiveness instead:

Yet Christian laws allow not such redress. (351)

[29] Earl Miner points out rightly that in his public character the Buzzard represents William of Orange—*Works of Dryden*, Vol. 3, p. 449, notes to lines 1120–94.

[30] Perhaps Burnet's publication of 'Reasons against the Repealing of the Acts of Parliament concerning the Test' may have angered Dryden—Miner, *Works of Dryden*, Vol. 3, p. 449, notes to lines 1120–94.

> But brought the Vertues of his Heav'n along,
> A fair Behaviour, and a fluent Tongue:
> And yet with all his Arts he could not thrive;
> The most unlucky Parasite alive.
>
> (III, 1147–56)

This witty, invective satire is reminiscent of Dryden's earlier poems, for example 'The Medal'; but by the strategy of having the Hind paint the picture, the poet not only creates a sense of his own objectivity but preserves his posture of humility while he has his revenge.

There is probably an element of personal malice also in the attack on Father Petres (or Petre) as the Martin, in the episode of the Swallows narrated by the Panther. Dryden assumes a posture of objectivity in the remarks to the reader: 'There are in it two *Episodes*, or *Fables*. . . . In both of these I have made use of the Common Places of *Satyr*, whether true or false, which are urg'd by the Members of one Church against the other: At which I hope no *Reader* of either Party will be scandaliz'd; because they are not of my Invention. . . .'[31] The Panther says to the Hind, 'Make you the moral, and I'll tell the tale' (III, 426). After the story, the Hind is incensed, 'For well she mark'd the malice of the tale' (III, 640). There is no doubt that the malice of the Panther (Anglicans) is exposed in the story; but the moral is more ambiguous, and we might assume that Dryden was also attacking Father Edward Petres in the figure of the Martin. . . .

Both the Hind and the Panther thus become effective instruments for Dryden's attack on people whom he found objectionable for one reason or another, and the use of satire gives incisiveness and witty pointedness to the exposure. The sympathetic persona of the Hind most readily permitted Dryden to attack his enemies, Stillingfleet and Burnet, while maintaining his posture of humility and charity. In a more devious fashion, the malicious Panther served to express Dryden's not heavily disguised censure of Father Petres. Yet these attacks sprang ultimately from Dryden's pride, that is, his lack of true Christian charity and humility; and the beast fable again provided Dryden a means for dramatizing the ever-continuing struggle to subdue his pride and achieve his goal of the true Christian spirit.

In Part III, the not always successful struggle of the convert to achieve Christian humility and to suppress his pride and desire for revenge is vividly presented in the debate between the Hind and the Panther. In the context of Dryden's attack on Stillingfleet, which is motivated by a desire for revenge, we hear the Hind's admonition to the poet to assume Christian humility:

> Be vengeance wholly left to pow'rs divine,
> And let heav'n judge betwixt your sons and mine:
> If joyes hereafter must be purchas'd here
> With loss of all that mortals hold so dear,

---

[31] Miner, *Works of Dryden*, Vol. 3, p. 122.

Then welcome infamy and publick shame,
And, last, a long farewell to worldly fame.
'Tis said with ease, but oh, how hardly try'd ⎫
By haughty souls to humane honour ty'd! ⎬
O sharp convulsive pangs of agonizing pride! ⎭
Down then thou rebell, never more to rise, ⎫
And what thou didst, and do'st so dearly prize, ⎬
That fame, that darling fame, make that thy sacrifice. ⎭
'Tis nothing thou hast giv'n, then add thy tears
For a long race of unrepenting years:
'Tis nothing yet; yet all thou hast to give,
Then add those *may-be* years thou hast to live.

(III, 279–94)

These lines are spoken by the Hind, but the sentiments are clearly the poet's own. In intent at least, the poet offers up his pride and worldliness on the altar of piety and Christian humility. But the 'sharp convulsive pangs' are there. After these words, the Hind addresses further words of admonition to the poet:

Thus (she pursu'd) I discipline a son
Whose uncheck'd fury to revenge wou'd run:
He champs the bit, impatient of his loss,
And starts a-side, and flounders at the cross.
Instruct him better, gracious God, to know,
As thine is vengeance, so forgiveness too.
That suff'ring from ill tongues he bears no more
Than what his Sovereign bears, and what his Saviour bore.

(III, 298–305)

In the vivid image of the steed champing the bit, starting aside, and floundering, the poet communicates the effort required to forgive his enemies in true Christian charity. At the same time, the poet partly negates the admonition; for in comparing himself to the King and even to Christ, he reveals his unconscious pride. Further, by using the Hind, the poet is able to admonish himself against revenge and also have his revenge, as the Hind goes on to castigate Stillingfleet (lines 306–40).

For Dryden, the main problem as a Christian was practical piety in daily life,[32] and this became a matter of achieving humility and charity in the face of bitter personal attacks by enemies.[33] When his poem was

[32] '. . . he expressed that aspect of religious experience to which we may surmise that, given the temper of his mind and of contemporary religion, he had devoted most attention after his conversion, daily personal piety'—Ruth Wallerstein, *Studies in Seventeenth-Century Poetic*, Madison, 1961, p. 142. The stress on charitable and moral conduct and on practical piety was in accord with the trend of religion in the late seventeenth century, which tended to identify religion with morality—G. R. Cragg, *From Puritanism to the Age of Reason*, Cambridge, Eng., 1950, pp. 47, 78, 129.

[33] For a list of works attacking Dryden, see Hugh Macdonald, *John Dryden: A Bibliography of Early Editions and of Drydeniana*, Oxford, 1939, pp. 254–8.

attacked, for example in 'The Hind and the Panther, Transvers'd to
the Story of the Country Mouse and the City Mouse' (1687), the
primary challenge was to be patient and humble, a Christian posture
extremely difficult for a belligerent and proud man like Dryden. A
vitriolic lampoon like 'The Laureat' by Robert Gould typified the kind
of personal smear launched against him:

> Thou stand'st upon thy own Records, a Knave;
> Condemn'd to live in thy Apostate Rhimes,
> The Curse of Ours, and Scoff of Future Times.[34]

These attacks on Dryden impugned his character rather than answered
the arguments advanced in 'The Hind and the Panther'.[35] Faced with
this situation, the poet continued to strive for the charity that would
help him forgive his enemies. In 'Britannia Rediviva' (1688), Dryden
touched on the same problem as in the earlier poem:

> Our Manners, as Religion were a Dream,
> Are such as teach the Nations to *Blaspheme.*
> In Lusts we wallow, and with Pride we swell,
> And Injuries, with Injuries repell;
> Prompt to Revenge, not daring to forgive,
> Our Lives unteach the Doctrine we believe;
>
> (279–84)[36]

Again, in the dedication of his translation of Bouhours' *Life of St
Francis Xavier* (1688), Dryden remarked: 'I am sure if we take the
example of our Soveraigns, we shall place our confidence in God alone:
we shall be assiduous in our devotions, moderate in our expectations,
humble in our carriage, and forgiving of our Enemies.'[37]

'The Hind and the Panther' is the most vivid statement of Dryden's
long struggle to become a true Christian. In the largest sense, the
entire poem is a dramatic presentation of the poet's intellectual and
spiritual struggles as a Christian. On one level, the Hind and the
Panther represent the Catholic versus the Anglican position on church
authority; but their debate is a dramatization too of the doctrinal doubts
that vexed Dryden's mind, and it re-enacts in the present moment the
intellectual battle waged within the poet before his conversion. The
Hind and the Panther also represent the true Christian spirit of
charity and humility of the Catholic Church versus the proud, worldly
spirit of the Anglican Church and its members. But in another sense,
the two beasts, the one meek and the other revengeful, represent two
aspects of Dryden's nature engaged in a never wholly resolved spiritual
struggle.

---

34 [Robert Gould], *The Laureat*, London, 1687, p. 1.
35 Charles E. Ward, *The Life of John Dryden*, Chapel Hill, 1961, p. 233.
36 From Miner, *Works of Dryden*, Vol. 3, p. 219.
37 Dominique Bouhours, *The Life of St. Francis Xavier of the Society of
Jesus*, tr. John Dryden, London, 1688, sig. A4.

Most effectively Dryden communicates a sense of the constant struggle within himself between pride and humility, between revenge and Christian charity, which is the practical expression of his piety. The Panther is as much Dryden as is the Hind: the proud, vindictive, worldly beast is the part of himself the poet tried so hard to suppress. In communicating the quality of that long and intense struggle to achieve faith and humility, Dryden succeeded as a religious poet: the personal agon of his embattled faith becomes the highest testimony to his Christian and Catholic commitment. Further, his personal drama becomes the pattern of the Christian drama, and the poem in true neoclassical fashion becomes a universal statement about every Christian's struggle to achieve charity and humility.

From 'The Personal Drama of Dryden's "The Hind and the Panther" ', *PMLA*, Vol. 87, No. 3, 1972, pp. 406–16 (406, 407–12, 413–16 [selected annotation]). The editors are grateful to Professor Fujimura for making this essay available to us prior to its publication and for allowing us to include it in an abridged form.

Select Bibliography

COLLECTED EDITIONS

The first complete edition of Dryden's *Works* was edited by Sir Walter Scott, 18 vols, Edinburgh, 1808. Scott's edition was revised slightly by George Saintsbury, 18 vols, London, 1882–92. The 'California' edition of Dryden's works edited by H. T. Swedenberg *et al*, 21 projected vols, Berkeley, 1956–, will be the standard edition. The following volumes are completed: Vol. 1: *Poems, 1649–1680*; Vol. 3: *Poems, 1685–1692*; Vol. 8: *Plays: The Wild Gallant, The Rival Ladies, The Indian Queen*; Vol. 9: *Plays: The Indian Emperour, Secret Love, Sir Martin Mar-all*; Vol. 10: *Plays: The Tempest, Tyrannick Love, An Evening's Love*; Vol. 17: *Prose: 1668–1691*. Dryden's *Poems* have been edited by George R. Noyes, Cambridge, Mass., 1909, rev. 1950—a modernized text but good notes, and by James Kinsley, 4 vols, Oxford, 1958, and a one-volume selection, London, 1962—a good text; his *Of Dramatic Poesy and Other Critical Essays* by George Watson, 2 vols, London and New York, 1962; and his *Letters* by Charles E. Ward, Durham, North Carolina, 1942, repr. New York, 1965.

BIBLIOGRAPHIES AND CONCORDANCE

Bond, Donald F., *The Age of Dryden*, A Goldentree Bibliography, New York, 1970.

Macdonald, Hugh, *John Dryden: A Bibliography of Early Editions and of Drydeniana*, Oxford, 1939.

Monk, Samuel Holt, *John Dryden: A List of Critical Studies Published from 1895 to 1948*, Minneapolis, 1950.

Monk, Samuel Holt, 'Dryden Studies: A Survey, 1920–1945', *ELH: A Journal of English Literary History*, Vol. 14, 1947, pp. 46–63.

Montgomery, Guy, and Hubbard, Lester A., eds, *Condorcance to the Poetical Works of John Dryden*, Berkeley, 1957.

BIOGRAPHICAL AND CRITICAL STUDIES

BOOKS:

Bredvold, Louis I., *The Intellectual Milieu of John Dryden*, 1934, repr., Ann Arbor, 1956.

Budick, Eugene, *Dryden and the Abyss of Light*, New Haven, 1970.

Ferry, Anne Davidson, *Milton and the Miltonic Dryden*, Cambridge, Mass., 1968.

Frye, B. J., ed., *John Dryden: MacFlecknoe*, A Merrill Literary Casebook, Columbus, Ohio, 1970.

Hamilton, K. G., *John Dryden and the Poetry of Statement*, St Lucia, Queensland, 1967 and East Lansing, Michigan, 1969.

Huntley, Frank L., *On Dryden's 'Essay of Dramatic Poesy'*, Ann Arbor, Michigan, 1951.

Jack, Ian, *Augustan Satire: Intention and Idiom in English Poetry, 1660–1750*, Oxford, 1952.

Jensen, H. James, *A Glossary of John Dryden's Critical Terms*, Minneapolis, 1969.

King, Bruce, ed., *Dryden's Mind and Art*, Edinburgh, 1969.

King, Bruce, ed., *Twentieth Century Interpretations of All for Love*, Englewood Cliffs, New Jersey, 1968.

Kinsley, James, and Kinsley, Helen, eds, *Dryden: The Critical Heritage*, London and New York, 1971.

Kirsch, Arthur C., *Dryden's Heroic Drama*, Princeton, 1965.

Miner, Earl, *Dryden's Poetry*, Bloomington, Indiana, 1967.

Moore, Frank Harper, *The Nobler Pleasure: Dryden's Comedy in Theory and Practice*, Chapel Hill, 1963.

Nicoll, Allardyce, *Dryden and His Poetry*, London, 1923, repr. New York, 1967.

Osborn, James M., *John Dryden: Some Biographical Facts and Problems*, New York, 1940, repr. Gainesville, Florida, 1965.

Price, Martin, *To the Palace of Wisdom*, Garden City, New York, 1964.

Ramsey, Paul, *The Art of John Dryden*, Lexington, Kentucky, 1969.

Schilling, Bernard N., *Dryden and the Conservative Myth: A Reading of 'Absalom and Achitophel'*, New Haven, 1961.

Scott, Walter, *The Life of John Dryden*, ed. Bernard Kreissman, Lincoln, Nebraska, 1963.

Smith, David Nichol, *John Dryden*, Cambridge, 1950.

Swedenberg, H. T., Jr, ed., *Essential Articles for the Study of John Dryden*, Hamden, Conn., 1966.

Verrall, A. W., *Lectures on Dryden*, Cambridge, 1914, repr. New York, 1963.

Waith, Eugene, *The Herculean Hero in Marlowe, Chapman, Shakespeare, and Dryden*, New York, 1962.

Ward, Charles E., *The Life of John Dryden*, Chapel Hill, 1961.

ESSAYS AND ARTICLES:

General

Benson, Donald R., 'Theology and Politics in Dryden's Conversion', *Studies in English Literature*, Vol. 4, 1964, pp. 393–412.

Emslie, McD., 'Dryden's Couplets: Wit and Conversation', *Essays in Criticism*, Vol. 11, 1961, pp. 264–73.

Feder, Lillian, 'John Dryden's Use of Classical Rhetoric', *PMLA*, Vol. 69, 1954, pp. 1258–78.

Parkin, Rebecca Price, 'Some Rhetorical Aspects of Dryden's Biblical Allusions', *Eighteenth-Century Studies*, Vol. 2, 1969, pp. 341–69.

Swedenberg, H. T., Jr, 'Dryden's Obsessive Concern with the Heroic', in *Essays in English Literature of the Classical Period Presented to Dougald McMillan*, eds Daniel W. Patterson and Albrecht B. Strauss, Chapel Hill, 1967, pp. 12–26.

Wallace, John M., 'Dryden and History: A Problem in Allegorical Reading', *ELH: A Journal of English Literary History*, Vol. 36, 1969, pp. 265–90.

On 'Absalom and Achitophel'
Freedman, Morris, 'Dryden's Miniature Epic', *Journal of English and Germanic Philology*, Vol. 57, 1958, pp. 211–29.
Guilhamet, Leon M., 'Dryden's Debasement of Scripture in "Absalom and Achitophel" ', *Studies in English Literature*, Vol. 9, 1969, pp. 395–413.
Jones, Richard Foster, 'The Originality of "Absalom and Achitophel" ', *Modern Language Notes*, Vol. 46, 1931, pp. 211–18.
Thomas, W. K., 'The Matrix of "Absalom and Achitophel" ', *Philological Quarterly*, Vol. 49, 1970, pp. 92–9.
Wallerstein, Ruth, 'To Madness Near Allied: Shaftesbury and His Place in the Design and Thought of "Absalom and Achitophel" ', *Huntington Library Quarterly*, Vol. 6, 1943, pp. 445–71.

On 'MacFlecknoe'
Alssid, Michael W., 'Shadwell's "MacFlecknoe" ', *Studies in English Literature*, Vol. 7, 1967, pp. 387–402.
Korn, A. L., ' "MacFlecknoe" and Cowley's "Davideis" ', *Huntington Library Quarterly*, Vol. 14, 1951, pp. 99–127.
Towers, Tom H., 'The Lineage of Shadwell: An Approach to "MacFlecknoe" ', *Studies in English Literature*, Vol. 3, 1963, pp. 323–34.
Wilding, Michael, 'Allusion and Innuendo in "MacFlecknoe" ', *Essays in Criticism*, Vol. 19, 1969, pp. 355–70.

On 'The Hind and the Panther'
Hamm, Victor M., 'Dryden's "The Hind and the Panther" and Roman Catholic Apologetics', *PMLA*, Vol. 83, 1968, pp. 400–15.
Miller, Clarence H., 'The Styles of "The Hind and the Panther" ', *Journal of English and Germanic Philology*, Vol. 61, 1962, pp. 511–27.
Miner, Earl, 'The Significance of Plot in "The Hind and the Panther" ', *Bulletin of the New York Public Library*, Vol. 69, 1965, pp. 446–58.
Miner, Earl, 'The Wolf's Progress in "The Hind and the Panther" ', *Bulletin of the New York Public Library*, Vol. 67, 1963, pp. 512–16.
Myers, William, 'Politics in "The Hind and the Panther" ', *Essays in Criticism*, Vol. 19, 1969, pp. 19–34.

On 'Religio Laici'
Chiasson, Elias J., 'Dryden's Apparent Scepticism in "Religio Laici" ', *Harvard Theological Review*, Vol. 54, 1961, pp. 207–21.
Corder, Jim W., 'Rhetoric and Meaning in "Religio Laici" ', *PMLA*, Vol. 82, 1967, pp. 245–9.
Fujimura, Thomas H., 'Dryden's "Religio Laici": An Anglican Poem', *PMLA*, Vol. 76, 1961, pp. 205–17.
Hamm, Victor M., 'Dryden's "Religio Laici" and Roman Catholic Apologetics', *PMLA*, Vol. 80, 1965, pp. 190–8.
Hooker, Edward Niles, 'Dryden and the Atoms of Epicurus', *ELH: A Journal of English Literary History*, Vol. 24, 1957, pp. 177–90.

On Other Poems
Mother Mary Eleanor, S.H.C.J., ' "Anne Killigrew" and "MacFlecknoe" ', *Philological Quarterly*, Vol. 43, 1964, pp. 47–54.

Hope, A. D., ' "Anne Killigrew" or The Art of Modulating', *Southern Review*, Vol. 1, 1963, pp. 4–14.

Tillyard, E. M. W., 'Ode on Anne Killigrew', in *Five Poems, 1470–1870: An Elementary Essay on the Background of English Literature*, London, 1948, pp. 49–65.

Vieth, David M., 'Irony in Dryden's "Ode to Anne Killigrew" ', *Studies in Philology*, Vol. 62, 1965, pp. 91–100.

Rosenberg, Bruce A., ' "Annus Mirabilis" Distilled', *PMLA*, Vol. 79, 1964, pp. 254–8.

Swedenberg, H. T., Jr, 'England's Joy: "Astraea Redux" in its Setting', *Studies in Philology*, Vol. 50, 1953, pp. 30–44.

Golden, S. A., 'Dryden's Praise of Dr Charleton', *Journal of English and Germanic Philology*, Vol. 103, 1966, pp. 59–65.

Wasserman, Earl R., 'Dryden's Epistle to Charleton,' *Hermathena*, Vol. 55, 1956, pp. 201–12.

Joost, Nicholas, 'Dryden's "Medal" and the Baroque in Politics and the Arts', *Modern Age*, Vol. 3, 1959, pp. 148–55.

Miner, Earl, 'Dryden's Ode on Mrs Anastasia Stafford', *Huntington Library Quarterly*, Vol. 30, 1967, pp. 103–11.

Peterson, R. G., 'The Unavailing Gift: Dryden's Roman Farewell to Mr Oldham', *Modern Philology*, Vol. 66, 1969, pp. 232–6.

Hollander, John, 'The Odes to Music', in *The Untuning of the Sky: Ideas of Music in English Poetry, 1500–1700*, Princeton, 1961, pp. 401–22.

Levine, Jay Arnold, 'Dryden's "Song for St Cecilia's Day, 1687" ', *Philological Quarterly*, Vol. 44, 1965, pp. 38–50.

On 'All for Love'

King, Bruce, 'Dryden's Intent in *All for Love*', *College English*, Vol. 24, 1963, pp. 267–71.

Prior, Moody, 'Tragedy and the Heroic Play' in *The Language of Tragedy*, New York, 1947.

Wallerstein, Ruth, 'Dryden and the Analysis of Shakespeare's Techniques', *Review of English Studies*, Vol. 19, 1943, pp. 165–85.

On the Criticism

Blair, Joel, 'Dryden on the Writing of Fanciful Poetry', *Criticism*, Vol. 12, 1970, pp. 89–104.

Kirsch, Arthur C., 'Introduction', *Literary Criticism of John Dryden*, Regents Critics Series, Lincoln, Nebraska, 1966, pp. ix-xvii.

Mace, Dean T., 'Dryden's Dialogue on Drama', *Journal of the Warburg and Courtauld Institute*, Vol. 25, 1962, pp. 87–112.

Sherwood, John C., 'Precept and Practice in Dryden's Criticism', *Journal of English and Germanic Philology*, Vol. 67, 1969, pp. 432–40.

Thale, Mary, 'Dryden's Critical Vocabulary: The Imitation of Nature', *Papers on Language and Literature*, Vol. 2, 1966, pp. 315–26.

Thale, Mary, 'Dryden's Dramatic Criticism: Polestar of the Ancients', *Comparative Literature*, Vol. 18, 1966, pp. 36–54.